D1163813

WEST GEORGIA REGIONAL LIBRARY SYSTEM
Dog River Public Library

POETRY ROCKS!

Modern American Poetry

"Echoes and Shadows"

Sheila Griffin Llanas

Enslow Publishers, Inc.
40 Industrial Road
Box 398
Berkeley Heights, NJ 07922
USA

http://www.enslow.com

"Poetry is an echo, asking a shadow to dance." —Carl Sandburg

Copyright © 2010 by Sheila Griffin Llanas

All rights reserved.

No part of this book may be reproduced by any means
without the written permission of the publisher.

Library of Congress Cataloging-in-Publication Data

Llanas, Sheila Griffin.
    Modern American poetry, "echoes and shadows" / Sheila Griffin Llanas.
        p. cm. — (Poetry rocks!)
    Includes bibliographical references and index.
    Summary: "Explores modern American poetry, including biographies of twelve poets such
as Robert Frost, Ezra Pound, and Langston Hughes; excerpts of poems, literary criticism, poetic
technique, and explication"—Provided by publisher.
    Library Ed. ISBN-13: 978-0-7660-3275-0
    Library Ed. ISBN-10: 0-7660-3275-2
    1. American poetry—20th century—History and criticism—Juvenile literature. 2. Poets,
American—20th century—Biography—Juvenile literature. 3. American poetry—Explication—
Juvenile literature. 4. Poetry—Authorship—Juvenile literature. I. Title.
    PS324.L63 2009
    813'.5409—dc22
                    2009011529

Paperback ISBN 978-1-59845-379-9

Printed in the United States of America
012012 Lake Book Manufacturing, Inc., Melrose Park, IL

10 9 8 7 6 5 4

To Our Readers: We have done our best to make sure all Internet addresses in this book were active
and appropriate when we went to press. However, the author and the publisher have no control over
and assume no liability for the material available on those Internet sites or on other Web sites they
may link to. Any comments or suggestions can be sent by e-mail to comments@enslow.com or to the
address on the back cover.

Every effort has been made to locate all copyright holders of material used in this book. If any errors
or omissions have occurred, corrections will be made in future editions.

♻ Enslow Publishers, Inc., is committed to printing our books on recycled paper. The paper in every
book contains 10% to 30% post-consumer waste (PCW). The cover board on the outside of each
book contains 100% PCW. Our goal is to do our part to help young people and the environment too!

Illustration Credits: Art Resource, pp. 9, 53, 119; Associated Press, pp. 21, 38, Clipart.com,
pp. 60, 104; Everett Collection, p. 65; Flickr, p. 110; Library of Congress, pp. 13, 25, 48, 69, 79, 90,
113, 125, 136; Shutterstock, pp. 1, 5, 12, 24, 32, 37, 47, 59, 68, 78, 89, 103, 112, 124, 135.

Cover Illustration: Shutterstock.

Contents

Permissions

"Not Ideas about the Thing but the Thing Itself", copyright 1954 by Wallace Stevens, from THE COLLECTED POEMS OF WALLACE STEVENS by Wallace Stevens, copyright 1954 by Wallace Stevens and renewed 1982 by Holly Stevens. Used by permission of Alfred A. Knopf, a division of Random House, Inc.

"This Is Just to Say" by William Carlos Williams, from COLLECTED POEMS: 1909–1939, VOLUME I, copyright © 1938 by New Directions Publishing Corp. Reprinted by permission of New Directions Publishing Corp.

"The Fish" and "To a Steam Roller" reprinted with the permission of Scribner, a division of Simon & Schuster Inc., from THE COLLECTED POEMS OF MARIANNE MOORE by Marianne Moore. Copyright © 1935 by Marianne Moore; copyright renewed © 1963 by Marianne Moore & T.S. Eliot. All rights reserved.

"I May, I Might, I Must" from THE POEMS OF MARIANNE MOORE by Marianne Moore, edited by Grace Schulman, copyright © 2003 by Marianne Craig Moore, Executor of the Estate of Marianne Moore. Reprinted by permission of Viking Penguin, a division of Penguin Group (USA) Inc.

"The Rum Tum Tugger" from OLD POSSUM'S BOOK OF PRACTICAL CATS, copyright 1939 by T.S. Eliot and renewed 1967 by Esme Valerie Eliot, reprinted by permission of Harcourt, Inc.

"Scrub," "Spring," and "Wild Swans," copyright © 1921, 1923, 1931, 1948, 1951 and 1958 by Edna St. Vincent Millay and Norma Millay Ellis. Reprinted by permission of Elizabeth Barnett, Literary Executor, the Millay Society.

"Buffalo Bill's". Copyright 1923, 1951, © 1991 by the Trustees for the E. E. Cummings Trust. Copyright © 1976 by George James Firmage. "here's a little mouse)and". Copyright 1925, 1954, © 1991 by the Trustees for the E. E. Cummings Trust. Copyright © 1985 by George James Firmage. "in Just-". Copyright 1923, 1951, © 1991 by the Trustees for the E. E. Cummings Trust. Copyright © 1976 by George James Firmage, from COMPLETE POEMS: 1904–1962 by E. E. Cummings, edited by George J. Firmage. Used by permission of Liveright Publishing Corporation.

"Medusa", "Knowledge", and "The Alchemist" from THE BLUE ESTUARIES by Louise Bogan. Copyright © 1968 by Louise Bogan. Copyright renewed 1996 by Ruth Limmer. Reprinted by permission of Farrar, Straus and Giroux, LLC.

"I, Too", "Harlem (2)", "Cross", copyright 1951 by Langston Hughes, from THE COLLECTED POEMS OF LANGSTON HUGHES by Langston Hughes, edited by Arnold Rampersad with David Roessel, Associate Editor, copyright © 1994 by The Estate of Langston Hughes. Used by permission of Alfred A. Knopf, a division of Random House, Inc.

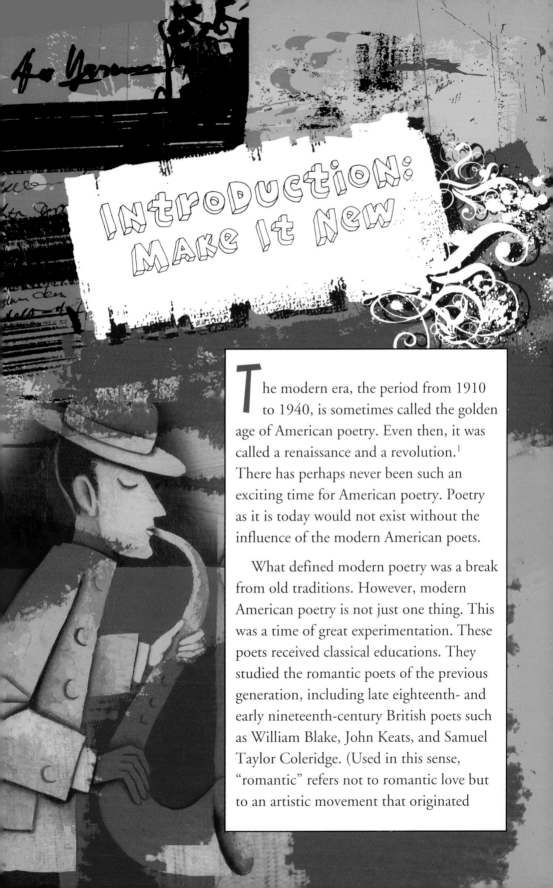

Introduction: Make It New

The modern era, the period from 1910 to 1940, is sometimes called the golden age of American poetry. Even then, it was called a renaissance and a revolution.[1] There has perhaps never been such an exciting time for American poetry. Poetry as it is today would not exist without the influence of the modern American poets.

What defined modern poetry was a break from old traditions. However, modern American poetry is not just one thing. This was a time of great experimentation. These poets received classical educations. They studied the romantic poets of the previous generation, including late eighteenth- and early nineteenth-century British poets such as William Blake, John Keats, and Samuel Taylor Coleridge. (Used in this sense, "romantic" refers not to romantic love but to an artistic movement that originated in the eighteenth century; it emphasized emotion, imagination, and an appreciation of nature.) But romantic poetry could not completely help them understand fast-paced industrialism and the threat of war. It was time for a change. This kind of break from tradition happens rarely. Little did the poets struggling in the 1910s and 1920s know that they were destined to make changes.

The Modern Poem and Free Verse

The first things to go in the poetry revolution were rhyme and meter. *Vers libre,* or free verse, took hold. Free verse was not entirely new. Two earlier American poets, Walt Whitman and Emily Dickinson, used free

FACTS

A pattern of rhyming words is called a rhyme scheme. Rhyme schemes are identified by assigning a letter of the alphabet to each sound at the end of a line. For example, in the poem "First Fig" by Edna St. Vincent Millay, shown below, lines one and three ("ends" and "friends") rhyme, so both of those lines are assigned the letter *a*. Lines two and four end with "night" and "light." They are assigned the letter *b* because they are different from *a* but similar to each other.

> My candle burns at both ends; (*a*)
> It will not last the night; (*b*)
> But ah, my foes, and oh, my friends— (*a*)
> It gives a lovely light! (*b*)

Thus, the complete rhyme scheme is *abab*.

verse. However, the modern poets had been firmly schooled in tradition. They never left end-rhyme and meter, mainly iambic pentameter, behind. Instead, they used meter more freely. Moderns such as Wallace Stevens, Ezra Pound, T. S. Eliot, and E. E. Cummings bent, shaped, distorted, and warped rhyme and meter in a way that electrified readers of poetry. In fact, because they simply changed rhyme and meter, T. S. Eliot insisted, in 1917, that "Vers Libre does not exist...."[2] He believed that all poetry had music.

Many of the principles of the modern poem were promoted by Ezra Pound. Basically, they are:

- use everyday language and common speech of ordinary people
- write in free verse, using new rhythms and rhyme schemes
- describe concrete images rather than abstract concepts

Wallace Stevens wrote, "There is such a complete freedom now-a-days in respect to technique that I am rather inclined to disregard form so long as I am free and can express myself freely."[3] The modern poets took delight in twisting tradition. Modernism radically changed what people thought of poetry, and the moderns knew it. Once tradition broke, each poet wanted to create his or her own style.

French Symbolism

When modern poets could not find poetry written in English that inspired them, they turned to other languages. The French symbolist poets helped set the groundwork for American modernism. Symbolism, a late nineteenth-century literary and artistic movement, represented ideas symbolically rather than realistically. Most of the modern poets in this collection were familiar with a book called *The Symbolist Movement in Literature,* written by the English poet and critic Arthur Symons (1865–1945).

In his chapter about French poet Jules Laforgue, a poet who influenced T. S. Eliot, Symons writes, "The old cadences, the old eloquence, the ingenuous seriousness of poetry, are all banished…. Here, if ever, is modern verse, verse which dispenses with so many of the privileges of poetry, for an ideal quite of its own."[4]

Words like this must have electrified and freed the young poets of the modern era. Symons's study of French symbolism encouraged free verse. It encouraged a use of slang and figurative common speech. This, at the time, was earth-shattering.

The Influence of Modern Art

Visual artists also had tremendous influence on modern poetry. In New York City, in February 1913, European modern artists, including Vincent van Gogh, Henri Matisse, Wassily Kandinsky, Pablo Picasso, and Edvard Munch, displayed new paintings in the International Exhibition of Modern Art. It was the first large exhibit of European modern art in America. Held in the 60th Regiment Armory Building, the show has come to be known simply as the Armory Show.

The show shook the art world and shocked art lovers. The poets loved it. William Carlos Williams is said to have laughed out loud when he saw the controversial cubist painting "Nude Descending a Staircase" by Marcel Duchamp. The painting tries to portray the movement of someone walking. In the exciting new expressions in art such as cubism, post-impressionism, and neo-impressionism, poets saw how painters shattered tradition. It was freeing. They wanted to take the same liberties with poetry.

The new art forms matched the new world. The First World War both interrupted and fueled the modernist movement. During and after the devastation of that war, artists in the United States and in Europe needed a way to express the chaos and alienation they saw and felt. Artists created fragmented collages with paint. Poets did the same with words.

Marcel Duchamp's "Nude Descending a Staircase," one of
the modernist paintings at the Armory Show of 1913.

Innovations in Print

Industrialization affected printing presses as well. Printing became easier than ever. Modern poets were the first to create "little magazines" that were devoted to poetry. One of the most important publications appeared in 1912. Called *Poetry: A Magazine of Verse,* it was edited by Harriet Monroe. She got a lot of help from her "foreign correspondent," Ezra Pound.

The typewriter was a new invention. Before, writers wrote in longhand. Printers set the type. Now, typewriters were used to create poems. Modern poets could place words and letters where they wanted on the page. This new control influenced the way they wrote. Even indenting lines was new. Poets could type visual, rather than spoken, poems. Paper was their canvas; they "painted" their poems.

A Community of Poets

The poets in this book were born before radio, television, and air travel. They drove horse-drawn carriages over hand-laid bricks, and they shared the road with pigs, cows, and hay wagons. They had coal and milk delivered to their doors. They lived through World War I, the Great Depression, and World War II. Most of them lived to see America become involved in the Korean War and the war in Vietnam. Some of these poets fought for civil rights and the women's movement. The changes they saw over the course of the twentieth century must have astonished them.

These poets knew each other and knew about each other. They studied together, helped each other get published, read and reviewed each other's books. They wrote letters to and about each other. They fought for and with each other, all for the sake of making a new poetry for a new world.

We hope this book will introduce you to modern American poetry. We were able to include only twelve poets, but there were many others writing and publishing during that same time.

A sampling of other modern American poets includes:

- Amy Lowell (1874–1925)
- Gertrude Stein (1874–1946)
- Mina Loy (1882–1966)
- Sara Teasdale (1884–1933)
- Robinson Jeffers (1887–1962)
- John Crowe Ransom (1888–1974)
- Conrad Aiken (1889–1973)
- Stephen Vincent Benét (1898–1943)
- Hart Crane (1899–1932)
- Allen Tate (1899–1979)
- Ogden Nash (1902–1971)
- Countee Cullen (1903–1946)

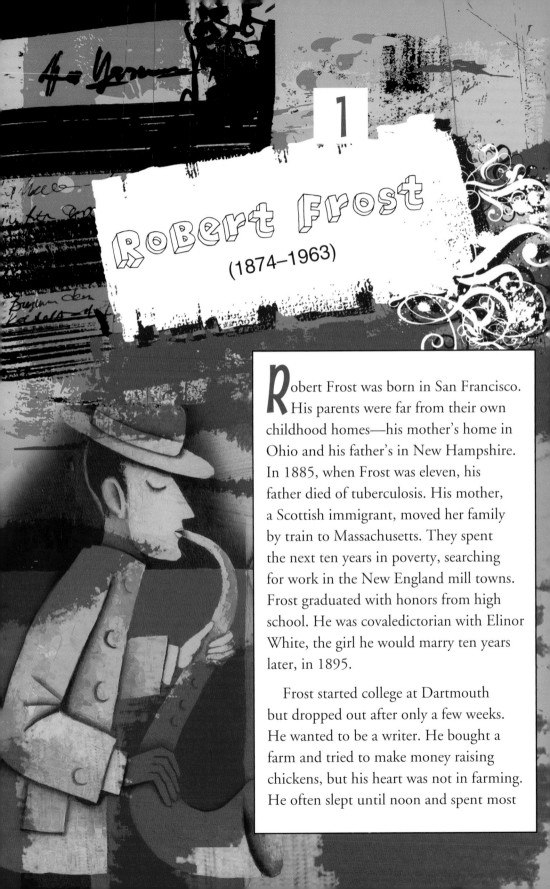

Robert Frost

(1874–1963)

Robert Frost was born in San Francisco. His parents were far from their own childhood homes—his mother's home in Ohio and his father's in New Hampshire. In 1885, when Frost was eleven, his father died of tuberculosis. His mother, a Scottish immigrant, moved her family by train to Massachusetts. They spent the next ten years in poverty, searching for work in the New England mill towns. Frost graduated with honors from high school. He was covaledictorian with Elinor White, the girl he would marry ten years later, in 1895.

Frost started college at Dartmouth but dropped out after only a few weeks. He wanted to be a writer. He bought a farm and tried to make money raising chickens, but his heart was not in farming. He often slept until noon and spent most

Robert Frost

of his time writing. A good teacher, Frost occasionally accepted teaching assignments.

By 1912, at age thirty-eight, Frost was frustrated by his lack of publishing success. He sold his farm and moved his family to England. In 1913, a London publisher printed *A Boy's Will.* Publishing in England allowed Frost to meet other writers, including Ezra Pound. During two years in London, he published some of his best-known poems. In 1914, *North of Boston* was published. Frost, now forty, finally became a well-known poet. When a New York publisher wanted to reprint his books in U.S. editions, Frost and his family returned home. He began teaching at Amherst College, then took a teaching position at Middlebury College that he held, on and off, until 1963.

He and Elinor were married for forty-three years, but they did not have an easy, happy life. Of their six children, only their daughter Lesley lived a long, healthy life. One son died of cholera. One daughter died at birth, another died giving birth, and another became mentally ill and was institutionalized. In 1938, Elinor died of a heart attack. Two years later, Frost's other son committed suicide. Frost, like many modern poets, did not reveal details about his personal life in his writing. His literary success may have helped him recover from grief.[1] At age forty-nine, Frost won his first Pulitzer Prize.

As he got older, Frost became America's most beloved poet. He remained active. He went to England in 1957, when he was eighty-six, to accept honorary degrees from Oxford and Cambridge. Frost became the first poet to read at a presidential inauguration when he recited "The Gift Outright" for President John F. Kennedy in 1961. He even traveled to Russia to speak with Premier Nikita Khrushchev and try to mediate between the Soviet Union and the United States. At age eighty-eight, the last year of his life, he was featured on the cover of *Life* magazine. He gave his last reading in December 1962. A month later, he died of a series of health complications.

The Runaway

Once when the snow of the year was beginning to fall,
We stopped by a mountain pasture to say "Whose colt?"
A little Morgan had one forefoot on the wall,
The other curled at his breast. He dipped his head
And snorted at us. And then he had to bolt.
We heard the miniature thunder where he fled,
And we saw him, or thought we saw him, dim and gray,
Like a shadow against the curtain of falling flakes.
"I think the little fellow's afraid of the snow.
He isn't winter-broken. It isn't play
With the little fellow at all. He's running away.
I doubt if even his mother could tell him, 'Sakes,
It's only weather.' He'd think she didn't know!
Where is his mother? He can't be out alone."
And now he comes again with clatter of stone
And mounts the wall again with whited eyes
And all his tail that isn't hair up straight.
He shudders his coat as if to throw off flies.
"Whoever it is that leaves him out so late,
When other creatures have gone to stall and bin,
Ought to be told to come and take him in."

Summary and Explication: "The Runaway"

"The Runaway," like many of Robert Frost's poems, seems to tell a simple story. The speaker and a friend find a colt that appears lost. The speaker and his friend talk about the horse. One guesses that the horse fears snow, is not winter-broken, ran away, and lost his mother. The other says that the colt's owner should come and take care of him. They can talk to each other but not to the horse. The horse cannot talk to the people. No one really knows why the horse is there.

The story the poem tells is full of tension and mystery. The reader sees the horse the way the speaker does. However, as in other narrative poems of Frost's, what we do not know outweighs what we do know. Who is the speaker? Who is the other person watching the horse? The reader never learns anything about the people in the poem—not how old they are, where they are going, or why they are in a mountain pasture.

In turn, the speaker knows nothing about the horse. "Whose colt?" the speaker (or the friend) asks, but the question is not answered. The people make assumptions about why the colt is there and what has happened. They cannot communicate with the horse. They simply observe an animal they believe is in trouble. They never find out what happens to the colt and, therefore, neither do the readers. The unresolved story leaves us with an unsettled feeling.

Poetic Technique

"The Runaway" is written in iambic pentameter, or five-beat lines. The twenty-one-line poem has a simple but uneven rhyme scheme. It is not a regular rhyme scheme. All of the end words except for "alone" are single-syllable nouns or verbs. Every end word does find a rhyme, but not always in the same order. The last two lines form a rhyming couplet, giving the poem, but not the story, a sense of finality. Because of the nice tension created by the rhyme and meter, the story in the poem is not allowed to run away, like the colt. The story is contained and measured.

Themes

As in other Frost poems, nature is a harsh reality. "The Runaway" takes place in early winter, as snow begins to fall. From the first line, the setting creates a sense of foreboding and loneliness, and of danger to the colt. In other poems, Frost describes a wall or fence to show that people are divided emotionally. In this case, a wall separates the speaker from the horse. The colt steps on the wall twice, trying to cross it. The wall could represent the divide between civilization and nature, between humans and animals. The runaway horse has managed to approach this border and get human attention. However, the speaker is unable to help or understand the colt.

In the poem's last line, one of the speakers says that the owner "Ought to be told to come and take him in." This last line of spoken dialogue sounds dismissive. It is the kind of thing people say when they are ready to move on. We never find out what happened after that.

As in other narratives, Frost simply presents the situation in "The Runaway." He does not solve the problem or take emotional sides. Frost lets readers think for themselves. The poem remains in your mind long after you read it. You want to work out the problem. What will happen to the horse? Why is the colt alone? Where is its owner? Should the speaker have tried to help the colt?

Discussion

Frost believed that good poems could be memorized. His poems are easy to remember because of their rhyme and meter. As you read the two following poems by Frost, "After Apple-Picking" (pp. 18–19) and "Fire and Ice" (p. 22), consider this: Are they deceptively simple, like "The Runaway"? What goes on under the surface of the text? What questions do the poems bring up?

After Apple-Picking

My long two-pointed ladder's sticking through a tree
Toward heaven still,
And there's a barrel that I didn't fill
Beside it, and there may be two or three
Apples I didn't pick upon some bough.
But I am done with apple-picking now.
Essence of winter sleep is on the night,
The scent of apples: I am drowsing off.
I cannot rub the strangeness from my sight
I got from looking through a pane of glass
I skimmed this morning from the drinking trough
And held against the world of hoary grass.
It melted, and I let it fall and break.
But I was well
Upon my way to sleep before it fell,
And I could tell
What form my dreaming was about to take.
Magnified apples appear and disappear,
Stem end and blossom end,
And every fleck of russet showing clear.
My instep arch not only keeps the ache,
It keeps the pressure of a ladder-round.
I feel the ladder sway as the boughs bend.
And I keep hearing from the cellar bin
The rumbling sound
Of load on load of apples coming in.
For I have had too much
Of apple-picking: I am overtired
Of the great harvest I myself desired.

There were ten thousand thousand fruit to touch,
Cherish in hand, lift down, and not let fall.
For all
That struck the earth,
No matter if not bruised or spiked with stubble,
Went surely to the cider-apple heap
As of no worth.
One can see what will trouble
This sleep of mine, whatever sleep it is.
Were he not gone,
The woodchuck could say whether it's like his
Long sleep, as I describe its coming on,
Or just some human sleep.

Frost's Poetic Style and Themes

Robert Frost holds a high place in American poetry, but his place among the modern poets has been somewhat of a question. He is a borderline modern, definitely a modern, and yet not a modern at all. His poetry, for one thing, always has rhyme and meter. Frost used traditional poetic forms. He wrote in traditional meter, using blank verse and rhyme. Rhyme and meter make poems easy to memorize. He wrote narrative poems and sonnets. He did not, as other modern poets did, break traditional verse. He did not use free verse.

However, he also used language of common people. Frost grew popular because his readers enjoyed what they perceived as homey, folksy, comforting poems. This was still new in poetry. After Frost became famous, audiences enjoyed the performances Frost called "barding around." He had a gentle stage presence that hid his troubled life. But Frost's poems could be dark. He described nature as merciless and cruel. With common language and dark themes, his poetry was very much in line with modernist principles.

Frost's long narrative poems, like "Mending Wall" and "The Death of the Hired Man," use elements of storytelling such as character and

FACTS

The Pulitzer Prize

The Pulitzer Prize, begun in 1917, was established by journalist Joseph Pulitzer to award Americans for excellence in newspaper journalism, literature, and musical composition.

Many of the poets in this collection received the Pulitzer Prize. Edna St. Vincent Millay was the first in 1923, followed by Robert Frost in 1924. Frost earned the Pulitzer four times. You can find a time line listing the winners of the Pulitzer Prize at its Web site.

Robert Frost receives the Congressional Gold Medal from
President John F. Kennedy in 1962. He had recited one of
his poems at Kennedy's inauguration the year before.

Fire and Ice

Some say the world will end in fire,
Some say in ice.
From what I've tasted of desire
I hold with those who favor fire.
But if it had to perish twice,
I think I know enough of hate
To say that for destruction ice
Is also great
And would suffice.

dialogue. Frost wanted readers to know exactly how his words would sound when they read them. Frost worked hard to find the right language to create the best sound. He explained it in a letter to a friend. "I … make music out of what I may call the sound of sense," he wrote. Frost could hear the music in dialogue. He knew how a conversation would sound without words. In his letter, he gives examples of lines such as "You mean to tell me you can't read?" and "Go down there and make those kids get out of the track."[2] Try saying those lines to yourself. Frost knew that readers would be able to hear the lines just as they would be said if they were spoken out loud.

What Critics Said

In 1912, Frost moved to England relatively unknown by American poetry readers. He returned in 1914 a celebrity. Robert Frost was awarded a total of four Pulitzer Prizes. No other poet or novelist has ever matched this. By 1947, seventeen colleges had given him honorary degrees, including Harvard and Dartmouth. He has been recognized and praised for being a true American poet in his descriptions of landscapes and people. He was not as experimental as some of his peers. However, Louise Bogan wrote that Frost, "although conventional, was original enough to further widen and diversify the American poetic scene."[3]

Major Works

North of Boston (1914)

Selected Poems (1923)

New Hampshire (1923)

West-Running Brook (1929)

Collected Poems of Robert Frost (1930)

The Lone Striker (1933)

The Gold Hesperidee (1935)

From Snow to Snow (1936)

A Further Range (1936)

Collected Poems of Robert Frost (1939)

A Witness Tree (1942)

Steeple Bush (1947)

Complete Poems of Robert Frost (1949)

Hard Not To Be King (1951)

Aforesaid (1954)

A Remembrance Collection of New Poems (1959)

You Come Too (1959)

In the Clearing (1962)

The Poetry of Robert Frost (New York, 1969)

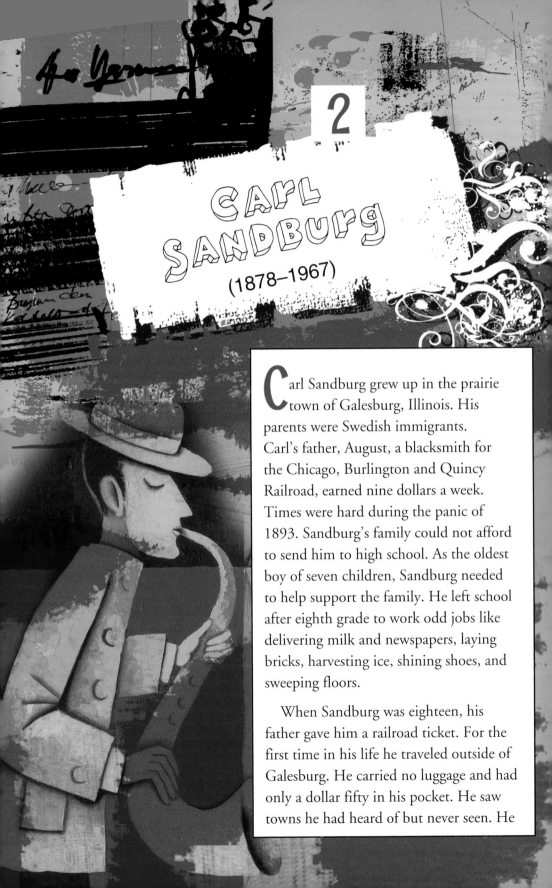

2

CARL SANDBURG

(1878–1967)

Carl Sandburg grew up in the prairie town of Galesburg, Illinois. His parents were Swedish immigrants. Carl's father, August, a blacksmith for the Chicago, Burlington and Quincy Railroad, earned nine dollars a week. Times were hard during the panic of 1893. Sandburg's family could not afford to send him to high school. As the oldest boy of seven children, Sandburg needed to help support the family. He left school after eighth grade to work odd jobs like delivering milk and newspapers, laying bricks, harvesting ice, shining shoes, and sweeping floors.

When Sandburg was eighteen, his father gave him a railroad ticket. For the first time in his life he traveled outside of Galesburg. He carried no luggage and had only a dollar fifty in his pocket. He saw towns he had heard of but never seen. He

Carl Sandburg

saw Lake Michigan for the first time. Most of all, he saw the bustling city of Chicago. It was his first taste of thriving industrialism. He loved it. He stayed three days, seeing as much as he could.

At age nineteen, this time with no ticket, he jumped into an empty boxcar and left Illinois for the first time. He rode the train to Iowa, Kansas, and Colorado, watching the landscape in awe. In each state, he worked odd jobs for a few days, as fry cook, carpenter, or wheat thresher. He slept under the stars or a bridge. Then he would move on. This was the life of a hobo. He kept a record of his travels in a notebook. Later, in his autobiography, *Always The Young Strangers,* he wrote, "I was meeting fellow travelers and fellow Americans. What they were doing to my heart and mind, my personality, I couldn't say then nor later and be certain. I was getting a deeper self-respect than I had had in Galesburg, so much I knew. I was getting to be a better storyteller."[1]

He served in the army during the Spanish-American War in April 1898, and was stationed in Cuba and Puerto Rico. His long letters home were published in the Galesburg newspaper. After his discharge, he enrolled in Lombard College in Galesburg, since tuition was free for war veterans. From 1899 to 1902, he wrote poems and newspaper articles. He got the education he missed as a teenager but never earned his degree. He spent two weeks in West Point, but he failed the math and grammar entrance exams. Travel fever struck again and he hopped a train to New York. By now, he had come to know the common, sometimes destitute people who traveled the country in boxcars, looking for work and better places to live.

In 1904, three small pamphlets of his writings were published. Sandburg married Lilian Steichen, the sister of the photographer Edward Steichen.

The couple lived in Milwaukee, Wisconsin. Sandburg was concerned for the American working class. He worked for the Socialist Party from 1908 to 1912, writing and distributing political pamphlets. He and his wife moved to Chicago, and Sandburg became a journalist for the *Chicago Daily News.* He covered politics, labor, and civil rights, topics he cared about for the rest of his life. The couple had three daughters. Lilian encouraged Sandburg to write poetry. Sandburg published some of his Chicago poems in *Poetry: A Magazine of Verse* in 1914, but poetry did not pay the bills. Sandburg began performing. He sang folk songs and played the guitar. He found that audiences were eager to hear his music. He collected more than three hundred songs, which he published in a book called *The American Songbag* in 1927.

Sandburg also wrote biographies. His book *Abraham Lincoln: The Prairie Years,* published in two volumes in 1926, was hugely popular. The four-volume sequel, *Abraham Lincoln: The War Years,* in 1939, earned him his first Pulitzer Prize. He earned another for *The Complete Poems of Carl Sandburg* in 1951.

In 1945, Sandburg moved his family to a peaceful estate in Flat Rock, North Carolina. Sandburg had a quiet place to write and walk and his wife had a place to raise her prize-winning dairy goats. The estate is now a National Historic Site, with home tours and five miles of walking trails. Sandburg became a beloved public figure. He appeared on television and radio. When he turned seventy-five, the state of Illinois declared his birthday to be "Carl Sandburg Day." He died at home in Flat Rock. On his request, his ashes were returned to Galesburg, his birthplace, and are buried under a red granite boulder called Remembrance Rock.

FACTS

First Names

Sandburg thought Carl was not an American name. He changed it to Charles. His Swedish father could not pronounce it, calling him Cully, a nickname that stuck all through college. Sandburg's wife convinced him to return to his given name, Carl.

Chicago

Hog Butcher for the World,
Tool Maker, Stacker of Wheat,
Player with Railroads and the Nation's Freight Handler;
Stormy, husky, brawling,
City of the Big Shoulders:

They tell me you are wicked and I believe them, for I have
    seen your painted women under the gas lamps luring the
    farm boys.
And they tell me you are crooked and I answer: yes, it is true
    I have seen the gunman kill and go free to kill again.
And they tell me you are brutal and my reply is: On the faces
    of women and children I have seen the marks of wanton
    hunger.
And having answered so I turn once more to those who sneer
    at this my city, and I give them back the sneer and say
    to them:
Come and show me another city with lifted head singing so
    proud to be alive and coarse and strong and cunning.
Flinging magnetic curses amid the toil of piling job on job,
    here is a tall bold slugger set vivid against the little soft
    cities;
Fierce as a dog with tongue lapping for action, cunning as a
    savage pitted against the wilderness,
        Bareheaded,
        Shoveling,
        Wrecking,
        Planning,
        Building, breaking, rebuilding,

*Under the smoke, dust all over his mouth, laughing with
    white teeth,*
*Under the terrible burden of destiny laughing as a young
    man laughs,*
*Laughing even as an ignorant fighter laughs who has never
    lost a battle,*
*Bragging and laughing that under his wrist is the pulse, and
    under his ribs the heart of the people,*
        Laughing!
*Laughing the stormy, husky, brawling laughter of Youth,
    half-naked, sweating, proud to be Hog Butcher, Tool
    Maker, Stacker of Wheat, Player with Railroads and
    Freight Handler to the Nation.*

Summary and Explication: "Chicago"

"Chicago" is one of Sandburg's many famous poems and one of the first he ever published. Dana Gioia calls it Sandburg's "signature piece … written in muscular free verse."[2] Sandburg first calls the city of Chicago names like "Hog Butcher," and "Player with Railroads."

At the time, immigrants flocked to Chicago, desperate for work and better lives. The city expanded with industry, which excited Sandburg. But at the time, factories often sacrificed people's safety. Sandburg addresses these problems in the first full stanzas of the poem. At the end, however, he defends the city. Sandburg loved the conflicting aspects of the big city. He loved the teeming throngs of people willing to give everything they had for a chance at a new life. Sandburg's own parents were immigrants, after all. His father worked for the railroad. Sandburg knew firsthand about the hard work it took to build a life in a new place.

Sandburg, who loved music, personifies Chicago—turns it into a character—and portrays the city as singing. He may have experienced the noises of the city as music, but the language of the poem sounds more like shouting. Richard Crowder wrote that "The hardest pounding of language in Chicago Poems had been in 'Chicago'…" There is a percussive quality to the poem, says Crowder.[3]

One technique Sandburg used to make a point was repetition. In the beginning of the poem, a reader may not know what to make of the harsh images on the page. Sandburg does not guide the reader's emotion. In the end, however, he returns to the beginning, and this time the repeated lines sound defiantly triumphant and proud. "Chicago" celebrates the city and its state of rapid industrialization and growth.

Limited

I am riding on a limited express, one of the crack trains
of the nation.

Hurtling across the prairie into blue haze and dark air
go fifteen all-steel coaches holding a thousand people.
(All the coaches shall be scrap and rust and all the men
and women laughing in the diners and sleepers shall
pass to ashes.)
I ask a man in the smoker where he is going and he
answers: "Omaha."

Carl Sandburg was a storyteller, historian, and musician as well as a poet. His home in North Carolina is now a national historic site.

Cahoots

Play it across the table.
What if we steal this city blind?
If they want any thing let 'em nail it down.

Harness bulls, dicks, front office men,
And the high goats up on the bench,
Ain't they all in cahoots?
Ain't it fifty-fifty all down the line,
Petemen, dips, boosters, sitck-ups and guns—
       what's to hinder?

      Go fifty-fifty.
If they nail you call in a mouthpiece.
Fix it, you gazump, you slant-head, fix it.
      Feed 'em....

Nothin' ever sticks to my fingers, nah, nah,
      nothin' like that,
But there ain't no law we got to wear mittens—huh—
      is there?
Mittens, that's a good one—mittens!
There oughta be a law everybody wear mittens.

Note: Sandburg used slang common at the time. Most of the slang terms in this poem refer to illegal activities: **petemen** are safecrackers; a **gazump** is a swindler.

Discussion

Sandburg's poems have a strong sense of "voice." How do the poems "Limited" and "Cahoots" sound to you? What voices do you hear? What about the poems' voices suggest that the vocabulary is casual, as if this is the speech of ordinary people?

Sandburg's Poetic Style

Sandburg heard language as music. Because he was raised by Swedish parents, English was his second language. He learned to listen very carefully to the way people spoke. He loved language that reflected the new industrialized cities. In his autobiography, *Always The Young Strangers,* Sandburg listed the sayings and phrases he overheard as a child growing up in Galesburg in his chapter called "Kid Talk—Folk Talk." For example, he jotted down the phrase, "Don't give me that guff." The word "guff" meant useless chatter. Someone who talked too big might be called a "manure-spreader" after the newly invented fertilizing machine. As the world changed, new language had to be invented.

Though Sandburg read many books, he did not make literary references in his poems, as many poets do. He wrote about real life. He was a nonintellectual. Harriet Monroe, editor of *Poetry: A Magazine of Verse,* observed that Sandburg had an instinct for poetry. She wrote, "He has a marvelously sensitive ear—he listens for his rhythms over and over and beats them out with elaborate care."[4] It makes sense that Sandburg's favorite poet was Walt Whitman. Both poets used expansive long lines, almost like prose, and wrote with an exuberant songlike celebration of life. Sandburg celebrated industrialism, but he also worried about its brutal effects on individuals. He watched people try to make good lives. He saw some people become trapped in lives that smothered their freedom.

Until the modern era, common people had been underrepresented in American literature. Sandburg brought hardworking Americans to life.

Just as industrialism was new, its portrayal in poetry was new for American readers. His poems were easy to understand and interpret, unlike some of the other poets of the time.

Sandburg did not only write about big cities. He also wrote about the prairie land where he grew up. Many of his first short poems, such as "Fog" and "Window," paint simple, spare, and lonesome images.

Sandburg did not use rhyme or conventional metric patterns. Instead, he often used repetition to provide structure in his poems. As a trained speaker, he wrote poems that reverberated like sermons. As a journalist and a biographer, he wrote literal poems that reported stories. As a singer, he wrote poems that sounded like songs.

What Critics Said

Sandburg's poems that first appeared in *Poetry: A Magazine of Verse* in 1914 outraged some readers. His writing did not seem like poetry to them. For one thing, he used slang. His was not typical poetic language. His images of slaughterhouses and railroad yards seemed harsh and ugly. "His vigorous colloquial language—a vocabulary that fits what it describes— shocked readers accustomed to finding elegance and grace in poetry," wrote Christopher Moore in the introduction to Sandburg's *Selected Poems.*[5]

When critics accused Sandburg of having no style, he responded by writing his poem "Style," in which he said, "Go on talking. / Only don't take my style away. / It's my face. / Maybe no good / but anyway, my face." Sandburg's style may not have suited every reader's taste. However, whether it was dark and gritty, or expansive and joyous, he definitely had a style all his own.

Without rhyme and form, critics did not know how to analyze Sandburg's poetry. Sandburg's voice was frank and simple. Because the poems seemed simple, critics thought they lacked meaning. His first book would become one of his most important in later decades, but when it first appeared, critics found it "brash, insolent, and shocking."[6] The critic Mark Van Doren loved Sandburg's short, imagistic poems and sense of humor.[7]

Sandburg's readers liked his second book of poems, *Cornhuskers,* better. By then, Sandburg had grown older. Now in his forties, he had softened his tone. Some of his poems were nostalgic memories of prairie life. This gave readers the tranquility they looked for in poetry. Besides, by now readers were growing used to free verse. By the time Sandburg's third book appeared, many critics and readers had grown to appreciate Sandburg. Some declared *Smoke and Steel* his best book.[8]

Major Works

Poetry

Chicago (1916)

Cornhuskers (1918)

Smoke and Steel (1920)

The People, Yes (1936)

Early Moon (1930)

Wind Song (1960)

Complete Poems (1950)

Prose

Rootabaga Stories (1920)

Abraham Lincoln: The Prairie Years (1926)

Abraham Lincoln: The War Years (1939)

Remembrance Rock (1948)

Always The Young Strangers (1953)

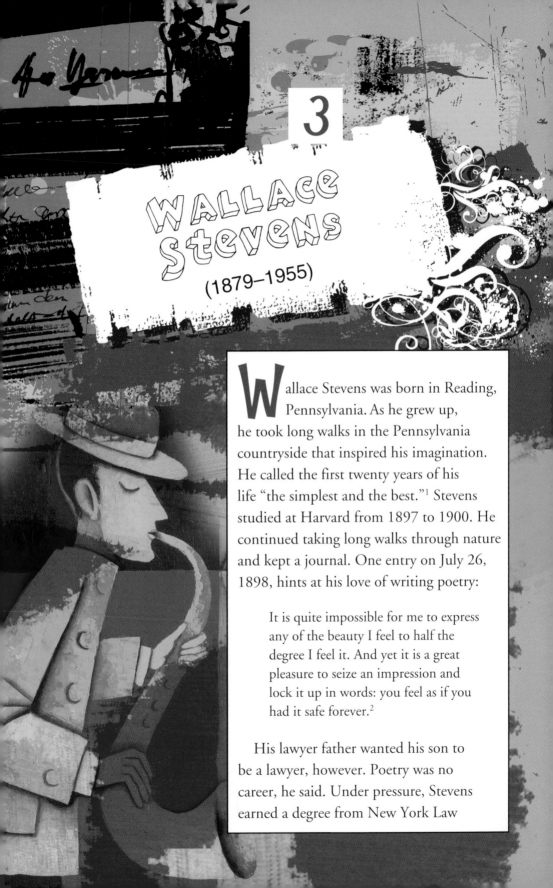

WALLACE STEVENS

(1879–1955)

Wallace Stevens was born in Reading, Pennsylvania. As he grew up, he took long walks in the Pennsylvania countryside that inspired his imagination. He called the first twenty years of his life "the simplest and the best."[1] Stevens studied at Harvard from 1897 to 1900. He continued taking long walks through nature and kept a journal. One entry on July 26, 1898, hints at his love of writing poetry:

> It is quite impossible for me to express any of the beauty I feel to half the degree I feel it. And yet it is a great pleasure to seize an impression and lock it up in words: you feel as if you had it safe forever.[2]

His lawyer father wanted his son to be a lawyer, however. Poetry was no career, he said. Under pressure, Stevens earned a degree from New York Law

School. Between 1903 and 1916, he practiced law off and on, but not very successfully. He enjoyed New York City, however, and socialized with poets like William Carlos Williams, Marianne Moore, and E. E. Cummings. He also wrote the poems that would form his first book, *Harmonium.*

Wallace Stevens

He fell in love with a Reading girl named Elsie Kachel, another choice his father disapproved of. Stevens may have allowed his father to direct his career, but he made his own decisions about love. After Stevens married Elsie in 1909, he never spoke to his father again.

Stevens published his first poems in *Poetry: A Magazine of Verse,* including his famous poem "Sunday Morning." But work came first. In 1916, Stevens took a job at the Hartford Accident and Indemnity Company. He and Elsie moved to Connecticut. Stevens became the vice president of the company in 1934. He worked there until he died in 1955.

To outsiders, it may have looked as if Wallace Stevens had a boring, solitary life. Having never learned to drive, he walked two miles to and from work every day. As it did when he was young, the motion of walking allowed his mind to wander. He composed poems while he walked, then dictated them to his secretary when he arrived at work. He worked all day at the office, and then walked home to read and write poems in the evening after dining at his desk. He led a life of quiet, disciplined routine.

This may have been partly why he and Elsie did not have a happy marriage. Stevens, like his father, did not express affection or emotion. He worked, studied, and wrote. He wrote letters to literary friends, but never invited them to his home. He loved Paris, French culture and language, but he never traveled there as so many of his peers did. He relied on the French postcards, books, paintings, and periodicals he got in the mail.[3] He traveled every year to the Florida Keys or Cuba. The landscape triggered his imagination; he describes it in many poems.

He published his first book, *Harmonium,* in 1923, when he was forty-three. Though it is now considered a work of genius, the book sold only a hundred copies and earned him a first royalty check of $6.70.[4] In the long run, however, it ensured his place in poetry. Wallace and Elsie Stevens's only child, a daughter named Holly, was born a year after Stevens's first book was published, in 1924. Stevens continued to write poetry and practice insurance law until he died of cancer at the age of seventy-five.

Not Ideas About the Thing But the Thing Itself

At the earliest ending of winter,
In March, a scrawny cry from outside
Seemed like a sound in his mind.

He knew that he heard it,
A bird's cry at daylight or before,
In the early March wind.

The sun was rising at six,
No longer a battered panache above snow . . .
It would have been outside.

It was not from the vast ventriloquism
Of sleep's faded papier-mâché . . .
The sun was coming from outside.

That scrawny cry—it was
A chorister whose c preceded the choir.
It was part of the colossal sun,

Surrounded by its choral rings,
Still far away. It was like
A new knowledge of reality.

panache—1. a bunch of feathers or a plume, especially on a helmet; 2. dash; swagger; verve

colossal—enormous, gigantic

Summary and Explication: "Not Ideas About The Thing But The Thing Itself"

It is hard to summarize "Not Ideas About the Thing But the Thing Itself." However, imagine watching the sunrise, hearing a bird cry, and writing a poem about it. Stevens may have been sipping his morning coffee when he looked out the window, heard a bird, and wrote this poem. The poem and its title seem to compare ideas of the mind with the reality of the world. In fact, you could study the title alone for a long time—and still not quite understand it!

The subject of the poem—a third-person "he"—hears a bird cry. For the rest of the poem the speaker tries to assert the conviction that a man actually heard a scrawny cry. The man is not quite sure he heard a cry, and if he did, he is not sure where the cry came from, whether from outside or within his own mind. He internalizes a sound from the outside world and finds out what happens when sound enters his mind.

By stanza four, the cry is "not from the vast ventriloquism of sleep's faded papier-mâché …" Stevens no longer focuses on *the thing*—the cry, or the sun. Now he pinpoints where the cry does *not* come from. The words of his own image have taken him to a new place. He now fully hears the sound of his mind. The definition of ventriloquism exactly suits the poem's purpose. The source of the cry has become abstract.

After each ellipsis, Stevens asserts that, yes, the sun is outside. That is certain. It has been proven. In the end of the poem, the speaker makes a profound revelation—the scrawny cry is part of the colossal sun. The revelation happens symbolically at dawn, as the sun comes up.

Poetic Technique

The poem's structure—six three-line stanzas, with three or four beat lines—does not have a noticeable rhyme scheme. As in many of Stevens's poems, the language has a lulling, internal rhythm. You hear the rhythm of his words inside. Stevens uses consonance and sibilance. He links a hard "cr" sound in s*cr*awny and *cry* and uses hard *c* and soft *c* sounds throughout the poem to create a crackling yet soothing sound.

Theme

The poem has a strange sense of time. It begins in the "earliest ending of winter." When is that? It implies that winter has more than one ending. Stevens pinpoints time in line two to the month of March. Later he says the cry happens at daybreak or before, and then at six in the morning. He continues to try, but comically fail, to pinpoint an exact time. This causes the poem to fall into a feeling of no time and also a profound beginning.

Stevens often wrote about reality and about the mind and about what happens when the two mix. The closing line is revelatory and at the same time flat. It is not that the scrawny cry *is* a new knowledge of reality; it is only *like* a new knowledge of reality. It is profound, humorous, and at the same time, deliberately flat. Wallace Stevens placed his poem "Not Ideas About the Thing but the Thing Itself" on the final page of his *Collected Poems,* 1954, the last book he would publish before he died.

Discussion

Stevens does not tell obvious stories. Think of his poems as you would paintings. What images come to your mind as you read "The Snow Man" and "Anecdote of the Jar"? What emotions do you sense?

Stevens's Poetic Style

Stevens's poems are not easy to read. His love of unusual words and his wit could make you go crazy trying to figure out what they are about. The poems are abstract meditations. They lull readers into deep receptive states with repetition and rhythm. Stevens's poems, like art, are to be experienced, not necessarily interpreted, but that does not mean they have no meaning. To notice his patterns and rhythms and language play is a way to find rich meaning in his poems.

The Snow Man

One must have a mind of winter
To regard the frost and the boughs
Of the pine-trees crusted with snow;

And have been cold a long time
To behold the junipers shagged with ice,
The spruces rough in the distant glitter

Of the January sun; and not to think
Of any misery in the sound of the wind,
In the sound of a few leaves,

Which is the sound of the land
Full of the same wind
That is blowing in the same bare place

For the listener, who listens in the snow,
And, nothing himself, beholds
Nothing that is not there and the nothing that is.

One way to enjoy his poems is to read them without expecting to find literal meaning. Listen to his language the way you listen to music. "The language must wash over you—you may understand very little but still be moved," says Christine Palm, a resident of Hartford and the president of "The Friends and Enemies of Wallace Stevens."[5]

Stevens's poems are rooted in philosophy, but they are not about philosophy. He never tries to instruct or educate. Stevens's poems are marked by an irony, as if the poet and the speaker of the poems are apart from one another. He loved puns and humor. Many of his poems, spoken by a persona with a heightened sense of voice, seem tongue in cheek. Many also describe nature and landscapes. Stevens loved to let his imagination roam free while he looked at nature.

He wanted his poems to be poems, nothing more. In an introductory note to his section in the *Oxford Anthology of American Literature,* in 1938, he wrote, "My intention in poetry is to write poetry: to reach and express that which, without any particular definition, everyone recognizes to be poetry, and to do this because I feel the need of doing it."[6]

FACTS

Stevens on Poetry

In 1942, Stevens wrote: "Poetry is poetry, and one's objective as a poet is to achieve poetry, precisely as one's objective in music is to achieve music. There are poets who would regard that as a scandal and who would say that a poem that had no importance except its importance as poetry had no importance at all. . . ."[7]

You can hear Wallace Stevens read his poems online at Hartford Friends and Enemies of Wallace Stevens.

Anecdote of the Jar

I placed a jar in Tennessee,
And round it was, upon a hill.
It made the slovenly wilderness
Surround that hill.

The wilderness rose up to it,
And sprawled around, no longer wild.
The jar was round upon the ground
And tall and of a port in air.

It took dominion everywhere.
The jar was gray and bare.
It did not give of bird or bush,
Like nothing else in Tennessee.

Stevens believed in the world of the imagination. He created a routine for himself that allowed him to spend hours lost in deep thought. He created metaphors for the unconscious, imaginative world.

He loved art, and used art to inspire his imagination. Some reports say he saw the famous Armory Show of February 1913 several times. He knew many artists and art collectors personally. Critics agree that he began writing his best poems when he applied the forms of modern art to his work.[8] For example, he loved cubism. He tried to write cubist poems. He wanted his words to have the fragmented effect on a reader that a cubist painting has on a viewer.

WhaT CriTics Said

Louise Bogan wrote, in a review of *Auroras of Autumn* (1950), "There is something theatrical in much of [Stevens's] writing; his emotions seem to be transfixed, rather than released and projected, by his extraordinary verbal improvisations."[9]

In her review of Stevens's *Collected Poems* (1954), Bogan wrote, "His ability to link the outer world of reality closely to the inner world of vision has been astonishing from the first." She also wrote, "He was the first modern American … to deal with the American scene in imaginative rather than purely topical or regional terms."[10]

Major Works

Poetry

Harmonium (1923)

Ideas of Order (1935)

The Man With the Blue Guitar (1937)

Notes Towards a Supreme Fiction (1942)

Collected Poems (1954)

Prose

Opus Posthumous: Poems, Plays, Prose (1957)

The Necessary Angel: Essays on Reality and the Imagination (1951)

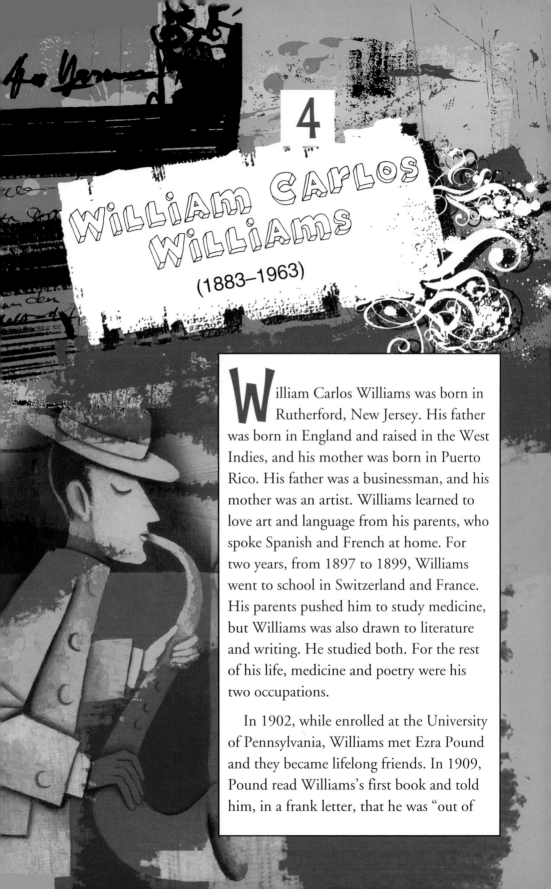

4

William Carlos Williams

(1883–1963)

William Carlos Williams was born in Rutherford, New Jersey. His father was born in England and raised in the West Indies, and his mother was born in Puerto Rico. His father was a businessman, and his mother was an artist. Williams learned to love art and language from his parents, who spoke Spanish and French at home. For two years, from 1897 to 1899, Williams went to school in Switzerland and France. His parents pushed him to study medicine, but Williams was also drawn to literature and writing. He studied both. For the rest of his life, medicine and poetry were his two occupations.

In 1902, while enrolled at the University of Pennsylvania, Williams met Ezra Pound and they became lifelong friends. In 1909, Pound read Williams's first book and told him, in a frank letter, that he was "out of

William Carlos Williams

touch."[1] On Pound's advice, Williams broke away from traditional rhyme and meter, applied Pound's imagist theories, and developed his own style. He also knew H. D., Marianne Moore, Wallace Stevens, and Edna St. Vincent Millay.

He had an artistic eye, which he used in his poetry. Like many of the poets of this era, he was a great art lover and knew many artists as friends. He visited the Armory Show of Modern Art in New York in 1913 several times. Some of the most shocking paintings made Williams laugh out loud.

In 1912, Williams married Florence Herman (he called her Flossie). They had two sons. Williams established a private medical practice in Rutherford. Many of his patients were poor or middle class. Money was tight during the Great Depression of the 1930s. Williams lost money in the stock market crash, yet he continued to treat his patients who were unable to pay. He worked overtime to pay his own bills.

In spite of his busy schedule, he continued to write. Even if he had only five or ten minutes between patients, he pulled out his typewriter and wrote. He wrote poems, plays, short stories, novels, and an autobiography. He published almost fifty books in his lifetime.

In 1951, after suffering a stroke, he closed his medical practice. He had developed a following of young poets influenced by his work, including such poets as Allen Ginsberg, Denise Levertov, and Robert Creeley. In his later years, he struggled to write in spite of health problems. He died in his sleep of a cerebral hemorrhage in March 1963, at the age of seventy-nine. Two months after his death, he was awarded a Pulitzer Prize for his final book *Pictures from Brueghel and Other Poems* (1962).

The Right of Way

In passing with my mind
on nothing in the world

but the right of way
I enjoy on the road by

virtue of the law—
I saw

an elderly man who
smiled and looked away

to the north past a house—
a woman in blue

who was laughing and
leaning forward to look up

into the man's half
averted face

and a boy of eight who was
looking at the middle of

the man's belly
at a watchchain—

The supreme importance
of this nameless spectacle

sped me by them
without a word—

Why bother where I went?
for I went spinning on the

four wheels of my car
along the wet road until

I saw a girl with one leg
over the rail of a balcony

Summary and ExpLication: "The RighT of Way"

The speaker drives down the road and witnesses one scene after another, then describes the first scene: a woman and a boy look at a man, who looks at the sky. Williams, if he is the speaker, looks at all three of them. In that way, the poem is about seeing. However, notice that none of the people in the poem look at each other or at the speaker.

Each image is still as the speaker races along on a wild, happy drive. "The Right of Way" demonstrates how Williams actively observed the world. His images stop motion like photographs or paintings, but the active speaker keeps moving, on to the next scene. Williams wrote about his observations, and his mind moved quickly along, on to the next image.

This poem ends with another scene, in which a girl slings her leg over a balcony. Williams does not say where the girl is going or what she is doing. The girl is certainly active, but Williams stops her in mid-action. She is caught in freeze-frame, as if someone took a photograph of her. The poem ends there. The reader is left with a sensation that something is about to happen but will never know what.

Poetic Technique

The poem's tone is joyous and exuberant. Williams takes so much delight in these images. Of course, there is a lot in each scene that he does not describe. Like an artist painting a picture, Williams chose which details to include and which to leave out.

Theme

Williams had a way of seeing images clearly as the world moved quickly around him. In the modern world, time sped up. Events happened fast. In certain moments, surrounded by chaos, Williams had the experience of seeing an image in stop-frame, clear, still, up close, and in focus. Those moments made an intense and significant impression on him. He wanted his poems to be like photographs.

The line "The supreme importance / of this nameless spectacle" echoes another famous line of his: "So much depends / on the red wheel barrow." Williams's poetry depended on concrete objects, on images. Objects were supremely important. In his poems, the objects and the people and the images he saw were *everything*.

The poem was published in the book *Spring and All* (1923). It is actually numbered XI. Williams freely alternated between writing prose and poetry. He gave the poems roman numerals.

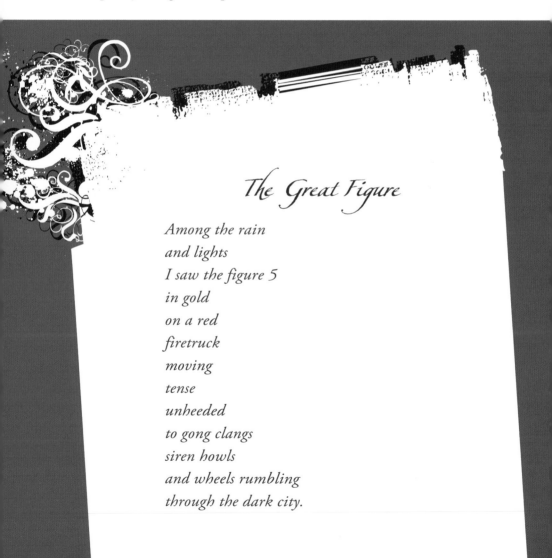

The Great Figure

Among the rain
and lights
I saw the figure 5
in gold
on a red
firetruck
moving
tense
unheeded
to gong clangs
siren howls
and wheels rumbling
through the dark city.

This painting by Charles Demuth was inspired by Williams's poem "The Great Figure."

Discussion

Williams wrote in his autobiography, "Once on a hot July day coming back exhausted from the Post Graduate Clinic, I dropped in as I sometimes did at [the artist Marsden Hartley's] studio on Fifteenth Street for a talk…. As I approached his number I heard a great clatter of bells and the roar of a fire engine passing the end of the street down Ninth Avenue. I turned just in time to see a golden figure 5 on a red background flash by. The impression was so sudden and forceful that I took a piece of paper out of my pocket and wrote a short poem about it."[2]

How does "The Great Figure" capture the chaos of the modern world? How is it like an abstract modern painting?

The Red Wheelbarrow

so much depends
upon

a red wheel
barrow

glazed with rain
water

beside the white
chickens.

WILLIAMS'S POETIC STYLE

Williams had a unique vision of the new modern poetry. Ezra Pound encouraged him early on to write imagist poems.[3] (Imagist poems focus only on concrete images.) Williams took to imagism easily because of his love of visual art. But he also wanted to use common American speech. This was a very new approach to poetry at the time. Poetry lovers were used to rhyme and meter and lofty subjects. Williams used words that were easy to understand.

In his poem "A Sort of Song" in 1944, Williams proclaimed "no ideas but in things." His poems represent "things" the way modern artists did, in order to present a new perspective on reality. Williams often placed things in relation to other things in his poems. The trunk of a sycamore tree, for example, is "between the wet / pavement and the gutter."[4] He arranged objects the way artists do when they paint. Objects and people, as in "The Right of Way," exist in relation to other objects and people but each is also alone and separate. Words were objects too. A poem did not simply represent an idea. The poem itself was also a thing, an object.

Williams wanted to make pictures with words from what he so intensely observed. The fixed outer image inspired his internal expression.[5] His mind moved quickly, and as he moved through the world, images came into clear focus and made a deep impression on him. Williams did not want his imagery to be symbolic or express a moral. He did not want the

FACTS

Multimedia

You can view William Carlos Williams's poem "The Great Figure" set to visuals. See the video online at "Spotlight on Voices and Visions."

This Is Just to Say

I have eaten
the plums
that were in
the icebox

and which
you were probably
saving
for breakfast

Forgive me
they were delicious
so sweet
and so cold

plums, the red wheelbarrow, or the sycamore tree in his poems to stand for anything. Williams did not want to see beyond, into, or through his images.

He did not want his images to be interpreted symbolically. He once wrote in his book *Spring and All* that "Crude symbolism is to associate emotions with natural phenomena such as anger with lightning, flowers with love ..."[6] He added that his poems of value would be "an escape from crude symbolism, the annihilation of strained associations."[7] He also used free verse. He believed that strict form, with rhyme and meter, would keep the work artificial and separate from reality. He wanted to break down the distinction between prose and poetry. Some of his books, such as *Spring and All*, mix poetry and prose.

As you page through his *Collected Poems*, you see many long, narrow poems. Williams's short lines are enjambed, meaning they carry over to the next lines. His sentences are much longer than his short lines of poetry. Some poems have no punctuation at all.

Like many modern poets, Williams learned a lot from Walt Whitman. He knew that Whitman was ahead of his time. Williams wrote, "Whitman's proposals are of the same piece with the modern trend toward imaginative understanding of life."[8] Williams is often compared to Whitman. Both poets used America as a theme. Both were fascinated with the human body.

What Critics Said

Some scholars and poetry lovers believe that Williams's poetry has been overlooked and not well understood. Early in the modern poetry era, Williams himself felt overshadowed by the work of T. S. Eliot. Eliot's work got so much attention that in 1922 Eliot's poem "The Waste Land" marked the very height of modernism. But Williams felt convinced that Eliot's work went against everything he believed in. It represented a step backwards, back to intellectual poetry that could only be read by scholars in universities. Williams thought Eliot was undoing all the work that modernist poets were accomplishing. In the 1950s and 1960s, however, younger poets, like Allen Ginsberg of the Beat Generation, turned to Williams as a mentor and for inspiration.

Major Works

Kora in Hell (1920)

Spring and All (1923)

Pictures from Brueghel and Other Poems (1962)

Paterson (1963, 1992)

Imaginations (1970)

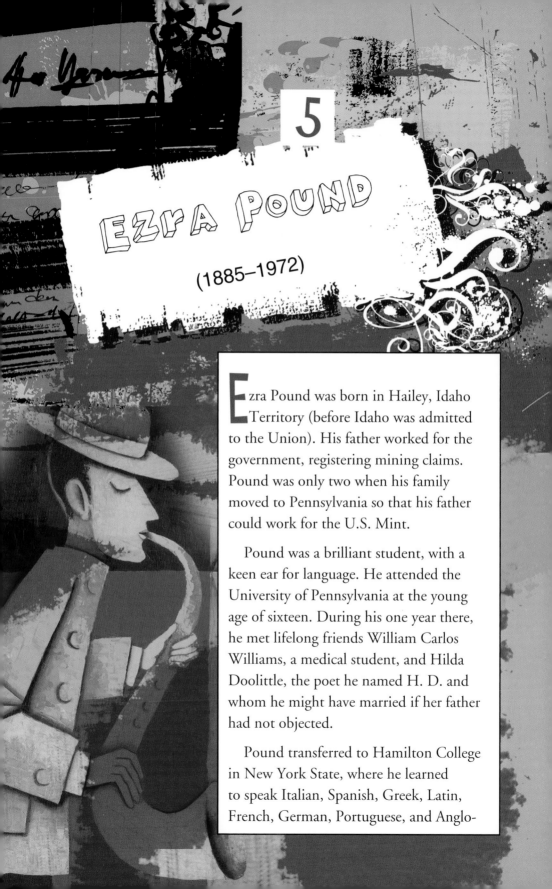

5

EZRA POUND

(1885–1972)

Ezra Pound was born in Hailey, Idaho Territory (before Idaho was admitted to the Union). His father worked for the government, registering mining claims. Pound was only two when his family moved to Pennsylvania so that his father could work for the U.S. Mint.

Pound was a brilliant student, with a keen ear for language. He attended the University of Pennsylvania at the young age of sixteen. During his one year there, he met lifelong friends William Carlos Williams, a medical student, and Hilda Doolittle, the poet he named H. D. and whom he might have married if her father had not objected.

Pound transferred to Hamilton College in New York State, where he learned to speak Italian, Spanish, Greek, Latin, French, German, Portuguese, and Anglo-

Ezra Pound

Saxon. At twenty-one, in 1906, he traveled to Spain and France. Then he returned to the University of Pennsylvania and added Provençal and Chinese to his list of languages.

In 1907, Pound got a job teaching at Wabash College in Crawfordsville, Indiana. One night, he let a stranded actress stay in his room. He claimed that she slept in his bed while he slept on the floor. But Wabash College fired Pound, offering him a year's salary to leave the college. Pound was relieved to escape Indiana. He took the money and returned to Europe. He published his first books of poetry at a very young age, beginning in 1908 with *A Lume Spento,* and, in 1909, *Personae* and *Exultations.* He lived in Europe for the next thirty-seven years, shaping modern American poetry from England, France, and Italy.

In 1912, Harriet Monroe began *Poetry: A Magazine of Verse,* one of the first small magazines that published only poetry. Pound enthusiastically took on the role of being the magazine's "foreign correspondent." In this role, he became the most influential writer of the modern era. He passionately urged Monroe to publish the poems and poets he liked. Monroe's memory of Pound was of his "gay and peremptory and violent letters, the vivid and slashing articles, the loud praises and protests—of all the sharp flashes from that very live wire ..." When she finally met Pound in 1923, Monroe was surprised that he was courteous and kind.[1]

In 1914, Pound married Dorothy Shakespear. The couple moved to Paris in 1920, and then to Italy in 1924. They had one child, Omar, in

1926. Pound had a daughter with another woman five months earlier. Pound began working on his lifelong project *The Cantos,* a group of poems that would eventually total 117. He spent more time on his own writing. He was influenced by the great Irish poet William Butler Yeats, and the two became friends.

In 1924, Pound moved to Italy. In 1933, he met Italy's fascist dictator, Benito Mussolini, and believed he would bring economic and social change. Pound wanted to avoid war. After World War II broke out, Pound began broadcasting fascist propaganda and making anti-Semitic remarks. In 1945, Pound was charged with treason. He was handed over to the United States and imprisoned in Italy for six months while awaiting trial. These stressful conditions may have led to a mental breakdown. In 1946, he was declared paranoid and unfit to stand trial due to insanity, and was committed to St. Elizabeths Hospital in Washington, D.C. During the twelve years he spent in the asylum, he continued working on his long body of work, *The Cantos.* In 1958, the treason indictment was dropped, and Pound was released from the hospital. He returned to Italy, and he died in Venice in 1972.

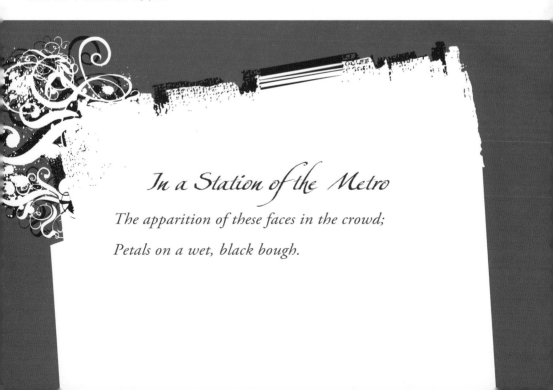

In a Station of the Metro

The apparition of these faces in the crowd;

Petals on a wet, black bough.

Summary and Explication: "In a Station of The Metro"

This short poem began with thirty-one lines. Using his imagist philosophy, Pound boiled it down to just three lines, including the title. Believe it or not, the poem took him a year to write. Imagism had three principles: "1. Direct treatment of the 'thing' whether subjective or objective. 2. To use absolutely no word that does not contribute to the presentation. 3. As regarding rhythm: to compose in the sequence of the musical phrase, not in sequence of a metronome."[2] Pound explained that the image, for him, represented the moment when an outward image became inward.

Every one of the twenty words that make up this poem provides information. The title describes the place—the Paris subway, which is called the Metro. The first line describes the crowd waiting at the subway platform—not just faces in the crowd, but the apparition of faces in a crowd. The word *crowd* implies an impersonal group of people. There are no distinct individuals in a crowd. The word *apparition* means a surprising,

FACTS

Pound on the "Metro"

Pound said this about writing one of his best-known poems:

Three years ago in Paris I got out of a "metro" train at La Concorde, and saw suddenly a beautiful face, and then another and another, and then a beautiful child's face, and then another beautiful woman, and I tried all that day to find words for what this had meant to me, and I could not find any words that seemed to me worthy, or as lovely as that sudden emotion. And that evening, as I went home along the Rue Raynouard, I was still trying and I found, suddenly, the expression.[3]

supernatural, or ghostly appearance. The word *apparition* elevates the line to mystery and poetry.

The last line, a delicate image made of six words, is complex enough to be analyzed. Rain makes fallen petals stick to the tough hard surface of a branch, perhaps the same branch that once supported the flowers in bloom. It is like an image from haiku.

The meaning of the poem comes from juxtaposing one image on another. These two lines could not be more different. The first describes a dark underground subway station, where there is almost no evidence of nature. The second describes the branch of a tree with no evidence of humans. What is the emotion of the poem?

Though the poem does not have a strict sense of rhyme and meter, it does have the musicality and delicate lyricism Pound promoted. *Crowd* and *bough* share the same vowel sound, so they are a slant rhyme. It could also be demonstrated, depending on how you read them, that each line has four beats.

A Girl

The tree has entered my hands,
The sap has ascended my arms,
The tree has grown in my breast—
Downward,
The branches grow out of me, like arms.

Tree you are,
Moss you are,
You are violets with wind above them.
A child—so high—you are,
And all this is folly to the world.

The River-Merchant's Wife: A Letter

(free translation of the poem by Li Po, from the Chinese)

While my hair was still cut straight across my forehead
I played about the front gate, pulling flowers.
You came by on bamboo stilts, playing horse,
You walked about my seat, playing with blue plums.
And we went on living in the village of Chokan:
Two small people, without dislike or suspicion.

At fourteen I married My Lord you.
I never laughed, being bashful.
Lowering my head, I looked at the wall.
Called to, a thousand times, I never looked back.

At fifteen I stopped scowling,
I desired my dust to be mingled with yours
Forever and forever, and forever.
Why should I climb the lookout?

At sixteen you departed,
You went into far Ku-to-en, by the river of swirling eddies,
And you have been gone five months.
The monkeys make sorrowful noise overhead.
You dragged your feet when you went out.
By the gate now, the moss is grown, the different mosses,
Too deep to clear them away!
The leaves fall early this autumn, in wind.
The paired butterflies are already yellow with August
Over the grass in the West garden—
They hurt me.

I grow older,
If you are coming down through the narrows of the river,
Please let me know beforehand,
And I will come out to meet you
    As far as Cho-fu-Sa.

Discussion

The poem "The River-Merchant's Wife" is written in the voice of a woman. As the title indicates, it is her letter to her husband, the river-merchant. That immediately gives the poem a great deal of intimacy. Pound was one of the first to translate Chinese and Japanese poetry. He published his free translations from the Chinese in his book *Cathay,* in 1915, and created a style that would influence many American poets.

Pound's Poetic Style

If there is one person without whom modernism could never have been the explosive movement that it was, it is Ezra Pound. He broke poetic boundaries in a way that may never be rivaled. He shattered the belief, at the time, that poetry could not or should not be translated. His linguistic

A Chinese painting. Pound translated poems from many languages, including Chinese.

talents led him, as Dana Gioia wrote, to "become the most influential translator of poetry in American literature."[4] Pound introduced Chinese and Japanese poetry to Western writers. Because Pound studied languages, he was able to read poetry many poets had never studied. These foreign poets influenced his poetry in a new way.

Early on, Pound found the romantic poets cliché. To him, they did not represent the modern world. His goal was to create a thoroughly new and modern school of poetry. "Pound was publishing critical essays frequently, using a variety of pseudonyms, in *The Egoist,* and generally setting himself up as the chief arbiter of taste for modernism," wrote Marianne Moore's biographer, Charles Molesworth.[5] Pound was the first, and for a short time the only one, to recognize T. S. Eliot's talent. If Pound had not insisted, Eliot might never have gotten published.

In 1934, Pound published his essays in a book called *Make It New,* explaining his new ideas about poetry. Pound even helped Yeats, whom he considered the greatest living poet, to use more contemporary language.

Even though Pound created controversy with his anti-Semitic remarks and his support of fascism, people recognized his brilliant and enormous contribution to poetry. Robert Frost appealed for Pound's release from St. Elizabeths Hospital. Marianne Moore was one of his most loyal defenders. In 1967, Pound apologized for his anti-Semitism in a conversation with the poet Allen Ginsberg.

WhaT CriTics Said

Pound spent twenty-five years working on *The Cantos,* a series of poems that spans eight hundred pages. *Canto* is from the Latin word meaning song. Some, including Pound himself, considered the poems a failure, a "botch."[6] Other critics, scholars, and readers consider *The Cantos* to be brilliant. Louise Bogan said that *The Cantos* "trace [Pound's] 'die-hard' character" and, "however brokenly, his development as an artist."[7]

Major Works

Poetry

A Lume Spento (1908)

Personae (1909)

Exultations (1909)

Canzoni (1911)

Umbra: Collected Poems (1920)

Homage to Sextus Propertius (1934)

Patria Mia (1950)

The Cantos (1972)

Prose

Gaudier Brzeska (1916)

Make It New (1934)

The ABC of Reading (1934)

Guide to Kulchur (1938)

Literary Essays (1954)

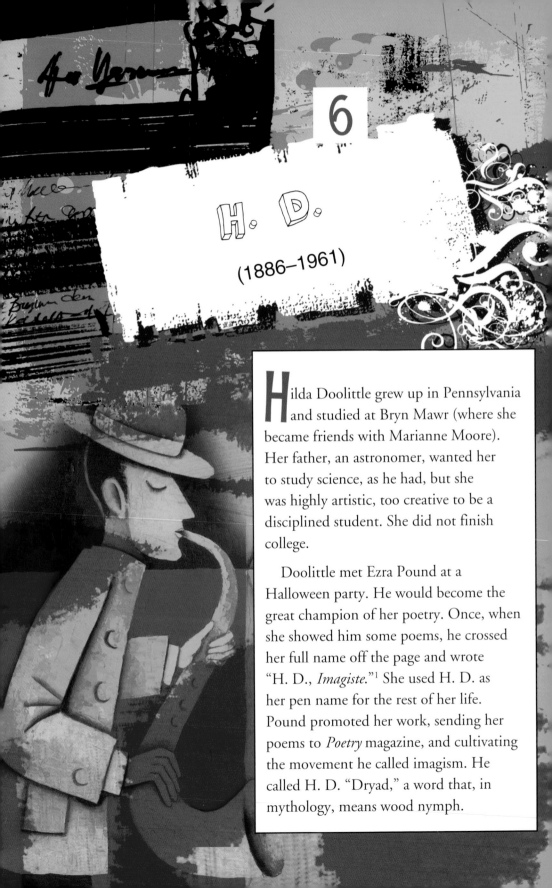

6

H. D.

(1886–1961)

ilda Doolittle grew up in Pennsylvania and studied at Bryn Mawr (where she became friends with Marianne Moore). Her father, an astronomer, wanted her to study science, as he had, but she was highly artistic, too creative to be a disciplined student. She did not finish college.

Doolittle met Ezra Pound at a Halloween party. He would become the great champion of her poetry. Once, when she showed him some poems, he crossed her full name off the page and wrote "H. D., *Imagiste*."[1] She used H. D. as her pen name for the rest of her life. Pound promoted her work, sending her poems to *Poetry* magazine, and cultivating the movement he called imagism. He called H. D. "Dryad," a word that, in mythology, means wood nymph.

Hilda Doolittle, known as H. D.

In 1908, Pound proposed to H. D. but was insulted when her father objected to the engagement. Pound moved to London, and wedding plans were dropped. Though H. D. was crushed (she wrote about her sadness in her autobiographical account *End to Torment*), she and Pound remained close lifelong friends. In 1911, she moved to London to live near him, in the community of other writers drawn to Europe. She published her first book, *Sea Garden,* in 1916. By then other poets were already imitating her imagist poems, including her friend William Carlos Williams.

H. D. married a poet named Richard Aldington. Their first child was stillborn. Aldington was an unfaithful husband, and the years he spent fighting in World War I kept them apart. The couple separated. H. D. suffered another loss when, in 1918, her brother was killed in action during World War I. Her father died in 1919. H. D. became pregnant again by another man. She broke off relations with both her husband and her lover. She had her daughter, Frances Perdita. At the time, she was living alone in a little apartment during London's flu epidemic. She survived in part because she was befriended by a woman named Annie Winifred Ellerman (1894–1983), a very wealthy novelist whom everyone called Bryher.

After these years of difficulty and struggle, H. D. fell in love with Bryher. She would be H. D.'s companion for the rest of her life. The two lived together from 1919 to 1946. H. D. acted in three films, *Wing Beat* (1927), *Foothills (*1928), and *Borderline* (1930, also starring Paul Robeson).

H. D. lived in London throughout World War II. Despite the Blitz—the intensive German bombing of the city—she wrote constantly. Her interest in the occult and astrology may have helped her to make sense of dark wartime events. After the war, in 1946, H. D. suffered a nervous breakdown. She spent the rest of her life living in hotels in Switzerland and Italy. She died in Zurich in 1961.

Garden

I

You are clear
O rose, cut in rock,
hard as the descent of hail.

I could scrape the colour
from the petals
like spilt dye from a rock.

If I could break you
I could break a tree.

If I could stir
I could break a tree—
I could break you.

II

O wind, rend open the heat,
cut apart the heat,
rend it to tatters.

Fruit cannot drop
through this thick air—
fruit cannot fall into heat
that presses up and blunts
the points of pears
and rounds the grapes.

Cut the heat—
plough through it,
turning it on either side
of your path.

Summary and Explication: "Garden"

The rose, in the first part of "Garden," is not a real rose, it is a rock rose. Not only that, but it is an image of a rock rose, an image that will never change, partly because it is rock and partly because H. D. has written it down. A rock rose cannot grow. It is solid and permanent. In the second part of "Garden," the hot air is heavy—so heavy that even fruit cannot move through it. The speaker asks the wind to change heat. She begs the elements to collide in order to make something change, ripen, or grow.

Poetic Technique

The images are metaphors; they stand for something. The simple, unadorned words of the poem—rose, rock, and tree—are symbols. They are symbols partly because they are unadorned. H. D. does not use adjectives to describe them. H. D.'s clear words have often been described as carved in stone, as "crystalline" and "chiseled." The rose and tree are not made specific with defining features. They are simply a rose and a tree.

Theme

The poems in H. D.'s first book, *Sea Garden,* share many images, such as the sea, gardens, and roses, and are worth reading as a group. The poems

H. D. and Freud

Psychoanalysis was a new science, originated by Sigmund Freud, known as the father of modern psychiatry. H. D. went to Vienna, where she was analyzed by Freud in 1933 and 1934. She wrote about her experience in *Tribute to Freud.*

are set at the edge of the ocean where water meets land. H. D. writes about the beauty that happens as a result of violent clashing of natural forces. Beauty can be destructive and destruction can be beautiful.

This poem may be about creativity, perhaps even creative limits. A garden is where things grow. But why does this ordinarily fertile and beautiful landscape seem so threatening? Why is there a sense of doom in the poem?

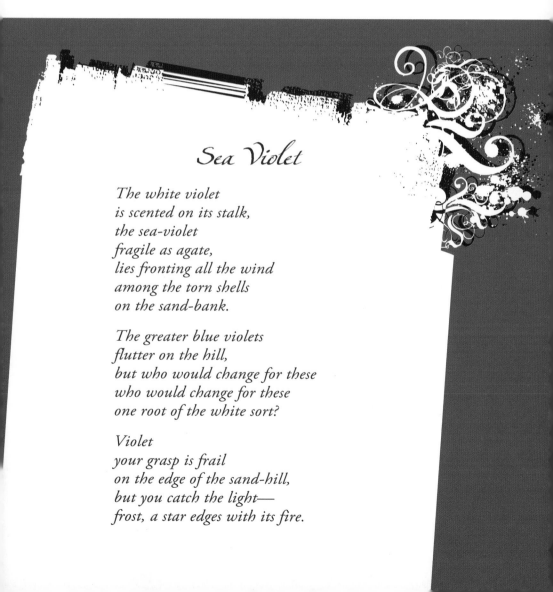

Sea Violet

The white violet
is scented on its stalk,
the sea-violet
fragile as agate,
lies fronting all the wind
among the torn shells
on the sand-bank.

The greater blue violets
flutter on the hill,
but who would change for these
who would change for these
one root of the white sort?

Violet
your grasp is frail
on the edge of the sand-hill,
but you catch the light—
frost, a star edges with its fire.

Orchard

I saw the first pear
As it fell—
The honey-seeking, golden-banded,
The yellow swarm
Was not more fleet than I,
(Spare us from loveliness)
And I fell prostrate
Crying:
You have flayed us
With your blossoms,
Spare us the beauty
Of fruit-trees.

The honey-seeking
Paused not,
The air thundered their song,
And I alone was prostrate.

O rough-hewn
God of the orchard,
I bring you an offering—
Do you, alone unbeautiful,
Son of the god,
Spare us from loveliness:

These fallen hazel-nuts,
Stripped late of their green sheaths,
Grapes, red-purple,
Their berries
Dripping with wine,
Pomegranates already broken,
And shrunken figs
And quinces untouched,
I bring you as offering.

Discussion

What do these poems have in common with "Garden"? How are the images and the style of the poems similar? What gives these poems a sense of timelessness or a sense that they occurred in ancient times?

H. D.'s Poetic Style

H. D. was an *Imagiste.* The imagism movement was shaped and promoted by Ezra Pound. The goals of imagism were to write short poems with high impact, to compress as much intensity into as small a space as possible. Using free verse, imagists focused on presenting concrete images, sometimes combining or juxtaposing different or opposing images. However, the poet provided little or no explanation of the images. The reader "looked" at a poem's images almost the way viewers look at a painting.

H. D. often described natural elements in her poems. She was good at combining opposing images. As we saw in "Garden," the sea can clash with land, wind can change nature. Some readers found her work "brutal" because the writing is intense and the images are treated harshly.[2]

H. D. was a feminist. She wanted to write as a woman and to write about women. Her model was Sappho, the ancient Greek poet. For most of her life, H. D. translated poems from Greek into English. She also wrote novels and an autobiography. Her experimental fiction is sometimes compared to that of Virginia Woolf.[3] H. D. combined imagist principles with the themes and styles of Greek drama and poetry. She used themes and characters from Greek mythology in her writing. This gave her poetry a sense of high drama and, like theater, a sense of persona or mask. She wrote spare lyric poems with pristine images. Every word was placed with perfect clarity.

What The Critics Said

H. D. was very respected by other poets. Pound, Stevens, and Eliot wrote important essays about her. During the 1920s, she edited *The Dial,* an intellectual literary magazine.

Harriet Monroe wrote:

> The amazing thing about H. D.'s poetry is the wildness of it. She is, in a sense, one of the most civilized, most ultra-refined, of poets; and yet never was a poet more unaware of civilization, more independent of its thralls. She doesn't talk about nature, doesn't praise or patronize or condescend to it; but she is, quite unconsciously, a lithe, hard, bright-winged spirit of nature to whom humanity is but an incident.[4]

There was a renewed interest in H. D. during the 1980s and 1990s. H. D. was surrounded by men as she tried to write from a woman's perspective. Many women scholars recognized how stifling her position was during the time she wrote.

Major Works

Poetry

Sea Garden (1916)

The God (1917)

Translations (1920)

Hymen (1921)

Heliodora and Other Poems (1924)

Hippolytus Temporizes (1927)

Red Roses From Bronze (1932)

The Walls Do Not Fall (1944)

Tribute to the Angels (1945)

Trilogy (1946)

Flowering of the Rod (1946)

By Avon River (1949)

Helen in Egypt (1961)

Hermetic Definition (1972)

Prose

Notes on Thought and Vision (1919)

Paint it Today (written 1921, published 1992)

Asphodel (written 1921–1922, published 1992)

Palimpsest (1926)

Kora and Ka (1930)

Nights (1935)

The Hedgehog (1936)

Tribute to Freud (1956)

Bid Me to Live (1960)

End to Torment (1979)

HERmione (1981)

The Gift (1982)

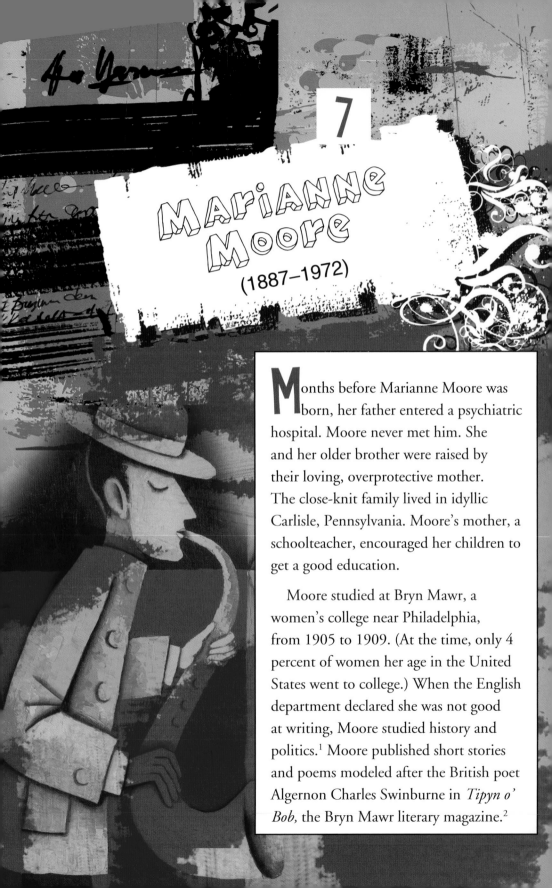

MARIANNE MOORE

(1887–1972)

Months before Marianne Moore was born, her father entered a psychiatric hospital. Moore never met him. She and her older brother were raised by their loving, overprotective mother. The close-knit family lived in idyllic Carlisle, Pennsylvania. Moore's mother, a schoolteacher, encouraged her children to get a good education.

Moore studied at Bryn Mawr, a women's college near Philadelphia, from 1905 to 1909. (At the time, only 4 percent of women her age in the United States went to college.) When the English department declared she was not good at writing, Moore studied history and politics.[1] Moore published short stories and poems modeled after the British poet Algernon Charles Swinburne in *Tipyn o' Bob*, the Bryn Mawr literary magazine.[2]

Marianne Moore

While at Bryn Mawr, Moore befriended the poet H. D. and the niece of novelist Henry James.

Moore's letters to her mother and brother were full of inside jokes, puns, and pet names. She also loved animals. She often included her jokes and animals in her poems. For example, one of her nicknames was Rat. (Her family all took names based on the children's book *The Wind in the Willows.*) She refers to it in poems like "To an Intra-Mural Rat."[3]

After graduation, Moore traveled with her mother to Paris and to London, where she purchased books by Ezra Pound. After they returned to Carlisle, Moore taught at the Carlisle Indian Industrial School from 1911 to 1915.[4] (One of her students was the Olympic athlete Jim Thorpe.) She joined the women's suffrage movement, attending meetings and handing out leaflets.

When her brother Warner, a clergyman, moved to New Jersey in 1916, Moore and her mother went to live with him. However, Warner just as quickly went to serve the war efforts, leaving the two women on their

FACTS

A Visit with Moore

Donald Hall describes going to Marianne Moore's apartment for lunch:

On a tray she placed three tiny paper cups and a plate. One of the cups contained about two teaspoons of V-8 juice. Another had about eight raisins in it, and the other five and a half Spanish peanuts. On the plate was a mound of Fritos, and when she passed them to me she said, I like Fritos. They're so good for you, you know. . . . She prepared a magnificent small cafeteria for birds.[5]

own. Though it seemed grim at the time, Moore and her mother moved to New York City, close to a buzzing poetry world. Moore loved it. She stayed in New York for the rest of her life, living in Greenwich Village and Brooklyn.

During her first years in New York, Moore worked half days at the Hudson Park branch of the New York Public Library, earning fifty dollars a month.[6] She liked her quiet life. Charles Molesworth, in his biography of Moore, suggests that Moore's image as a poet was the opposite of that of free-living Edna St. Vincent Millay.[7] Moore published poems in *Poetry* and *The Egoist*. In spite of her reserve, Moore made friends with other poets. Pound liked her poems and began to write to her.[8] In 1919, Moore wrote to Pound, "I like New York, the little quiet part of it in which my mother and I live. I like to see the tops of the masts from our door and to go to the wharf and look at the craft on the river."[9] In 1921, after reviewing T. S. Eliot's book *The Sacred Wood,* she also began to correspond with him.[10] In 1921, without Moore's knowledge, the poet H. D. printed Moore's twenty-four published poems in a book called *Poems*.[11] Moore later expanded the book to fifty-three poems and published it in 1924 with the title *Observations*.

Moore lived with her mother her whole life. She never married. She learned a sense of manners and propriety from her mother. She often revised her poems based on her mother's suggestions. Moore kept her signature sense of fashion all her life. As she grew older, people on the street recognized her in her black cape and tricorn hat, over red hair braided and wound around her head.

In 1947, Moore's beloved mother died. Moore was sixty, and over the next decades, she became something of a pop-culture celebrity. She was friends with the boxer Muhammad Ali. She threw the first ball at Yankee Stadium one opening day. In June 1966, she was on the cover of *Esquire* magazine. She appeared on *The Tonight Show* with Johnny Carson. Marianne Moore continued to live in New York until she died peacefully in her sleep in 1972.

The Fish

wade
through black jade.
  Of the crow-blue mussel shells, one keeps
  adjusting the ash-heaps;
    opening and shutting itself like

an
injured fan.
  The barnacles which encrust the side
  of the wave, cannot hide
    there for the submerged shafts of the

sun,
split like spun
  glass, move themselves with spotlight swiftness
  into the crevices—
    in and out, illuminating

the
turquoise sea
  of bodies. The water drives a wedge
  of iron throught the iron edge
    of the cliff; whereupon the stars,

pink
rice-grains, ink-
  bespattered jelly fish, crabs like green
  lilies, and submarine
    toadstools, slide each on the other.

All
external
  marks of abuse are present on this
  defiant edifice—
    all the physical features of

ac-
cident—lack
  of cornice, dynamite grooves, burns, and
  hatchet strokes, these things stand
    out on it; the chasm-side is

dead.
Repeated
  evidence has proved that it can live
  on what can not revive
    its youth. The sea grows old in it.

Summary and Explication: "The Fish"

The title of Moore's poem "The Fish" also serves as the poem's first words, proving them plural, not singular. However, after the title, Moore never refers to fish again. The poem is not about fish but about the ocean's depths. After the title, the poem moves quickly from one subject to another, from the fish in the title to mussel shells, barnacles, water, and other sea creatures. In fact, it is hard to keep track of Moore's subject.

There is no human presence in the poem. There is no "I" speaker or any description of human life. The poem describes a submerged world where many life-forms coexist. Though the words of the poem are lyrical and beautiful, Moore describes potential for harm undersea. Many images portray injury—an injured fan, a wedge of iron, the scarred cliff. Many critics have noticed how the bright imagery of "The Fish" contrasts with its dark content. Donald Hall wrote that "The Fish" deals "with the content lurking deep under the surfaces but is expressed in images that come from these depths."[12]

Poetic Technique

Some critics have compared the structure of "The Fish" to cubist art.[13] The poem has a syllabic structure typical of Moore. Each line and each stanza have the same number of syllables. The stanzas in "The Fish" each have six lines with syllables of 1, 3, 8, 1, 6, 8. The rhyme scheme is *aabccd.* The line breaks are unexpected and abrupt. The first rhyme scheme, repeated in lines one and two of each stanza, arrives quickly—"*wade* / through black *jade.*" The stanzas are almost impossible to read smoothly. Wallace Stevens, who reviewed her book *Observations,* wrote, "The lines move with the rhythm of sea-fans waving to and fro under water."[14]

Moore had the quirky habit of editing her poems continuously. For her, a published poem was not carved in stone. "The Fish" appears in different forms in various books. The version printed here is the original version from *Observations.* Moore changed "The Fish" for her *Collected Poems* by moving a single-syllable fourth line to the end of the third line, reducing the stanzas from six lines to five.

Theme

The poem's meaning is as murky and obscure as the ocean. The ocean may symbolize the unknown, the unconscious. The poem may be trying to capture the paradox of nature's seeming cruelty at the same time that it is teeming with life.

Donald Hall claims that "The Fish" is his favorite poem of Moore's even though, as he writes, "I do not fully understand this poem. … The last lines … are moving without being entirely penetrable."[15] One way to appreciate "The Fish" is to read it several times and focus on one element each time. Pay attention to her word choice. Track her subjects as she moves from the fish to the defiant edifice of the undersea cliff. Visualize her imagery. As you do, you will develop your own sense of her content.

I May, I Might, I Must

If you will tell me why the fen
appears impassable, I then
will tell you why I think that I
can get across it if I try.

fen—a marsh

Discussion

The poem "I May, I Might, I Must" is one of the few Moore published from her college years. "This poem with its theme of willed endurance, is particularly moving, I think, when one knows that it was written during those confused and homesick years," writes Donald Hall.[16]

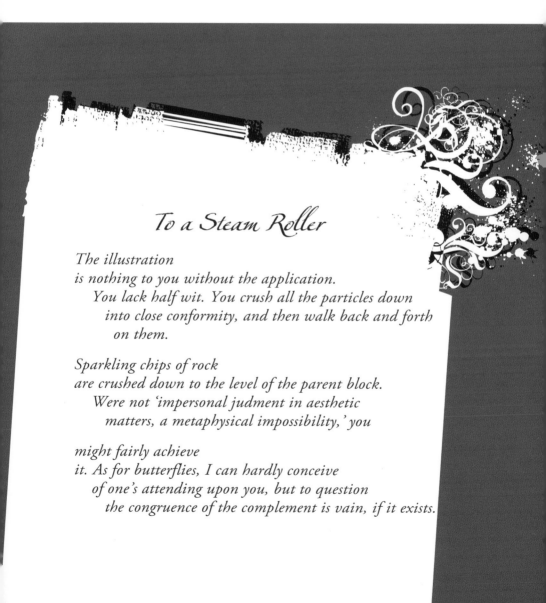

To a Steam Roller

The illustration
is nothing to you without the application.
  You lack half wit. You crush all the particles down
    into close conformity, and then walk back and forth
      on them.

Sparkling chips of rock
are crushed down to the level of the parent block.
  Were not 'impersonal judgment in aesthetic
    matters, a metaphysical impossibility,' you

might fairly achieve
it. As for butterflies, I can hardly conceive
  of one's attending upon you, but to question
    the congruence of the complement is vain, if it exists.

Discussion

"To a Steam Roller" is similar in form to "The Fish." It was first published in *The Egoist*. Notice how Moore crafts her rhyme scheme. Notice her trademark inclusion of a quotation. Be aware, as you read the poem, that Moore uses the steam roller as a metaphor for some of her harsher critics. How does that shape your interpretation?

Moore's Poetic Style

Moore developed a scientific fascination for animals when she was a child. Many of her poems are about animals. Many poems vividly describe nature. Since Moore observed life keenly, she gave her first book a fitting title: *Observations*. Elizabeth Bishop called Moore, "The World's Greatest Living Observer."[17] Her poems are intelligent and unsentimental. They are often about the collision of nature and culture. Images of nature are symbols and metaphors for her experiences of life.

Moore had a dry sense of humor. Her poems can have an ironic or satiric edge. Moore's poems are often called associative. She was good at combining ideas, placing one idea next to another. She sprinkled her writing with quotations. Her Bryn Mawr professors rejected that style of thinking and writing. However, that associative style was typical of the fragmented collage style of modernism. Moore called it "hybrid composition."[18] Ezra Pound admired Moore's work. In 1918, after she published her first book, Pound wrote, "You will never sell more than five hundred copies, as your work demands mental attention."[19]

Moore's writing habits were disciplined and focused. Her poetry reflects her manner. The writing is controlled, her language precise. She makes sure every word is exact. Her images focus around a central idea, giving the poems meaning, but many of Moore's readers simply love her language.

Moore sometimes created complicated forms—for example, patterns in which each line or stanza contained an equal number of syllables. She also used irregular and hidden rhyme schemes. The rhymed words in her poems sometimes appear unexpectedly. Donald Hall commented, "Eliot calls this 'light rhyme' and says that Miss Moore is its greatest living master."[20]

Moore edited her work almost severely. Sometimes, the minute she received a copy of her published work, she made changes before sending it to family and friends. Immediately after *Collected Poems* was published in 1951, she began editing some of her poems.

Her famous poem, "Poetry," which begins with the line "I too, dislike it," had thirteen lines when it was first published in *Observations.* Then, in *Selected Poems,* the poem had thirty-five lines. In *Complete Poems,* it appears with only four lines. In order to study Marianne Moore, scholars look at several versions of her poems. Moore was aware of her editing habit. She added this note to the first page of her *Complete Poems:* "Omissions are not accidents."

What Critics Said

Many of Moore's first readers loved her originality, her brilliant ideas, and her precise, condensed language. Others, however, saw Moore's poetry as brilliantly crafted but emotionless and cold. They thought her work lacked feeling. T. S. Eliot defended Moore's poetry in 1935, in his introduction to her *Selected Poems.* He said her poems "form part of the small body of durable poetry written in our time."[21]

Louise Bogan wrote, "[Moore's] insight often struck close to the heart of things; she could delineate with the precision of a miniaturist, and subsequently raise the most curious and fine of her pictures to a higher power, by relating them directly to abstract truth."[22]

Major Works

Poetry

> *Poems (1921)*
>
> *Observations (1924)*
>
> *Selected Poems (1935)*
>
> *The Pangolin and Other Verse (1936)*
>
> *What Are Years? (1941)*
>
> *Nevertheless (1944)*
>
> *A Face (1949)*
>
> *Like a Bulwark (1956)*
>
> *O to Be a Dragon (1959)*
>
> *The Arctic Fox (1964)*
>
> *Tell Me, Tell Me (1966)*
>
> *The Complete Poems of Marianne Moore (1967)*

Prose

> *Predilections (1955)*
>
> *A Marianne Moore Reader (1961)*
>
> *The Complete Prose of Marianne Moore (1987)*
>
> *The Selected Letters of Marianne Moore (1997)*

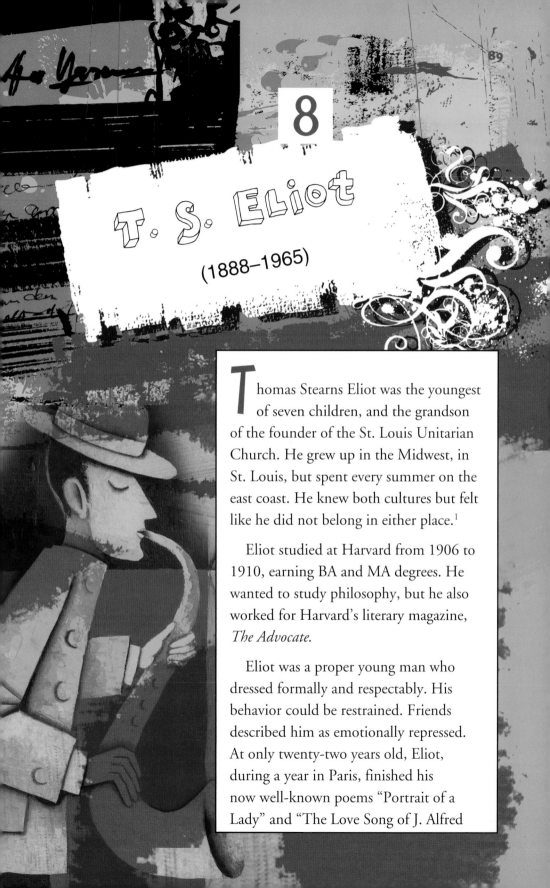

8

T. S. Eliot

(1888–1965)

Thomas Stearns Eliot was the youngest of seven children, and the grandson of the founder of the St. Louis Unitarian Church. He grew up in the Midwest, in St. Louis, but spent every summer on the east coast. He knew both cultures but felt like he did not belong in either place.[1]

Eliot studied at Harvard from 1906 to 1910, earning BA and MA degrees. He wanted to study philosophy, but he also worked for Harvard's literary magazine, *The Advocate.*

Eliot was a proper young man who dressed formally and respectably. His behavior could be restrained. Friends described him as emotionally repressed. At only twenty-two years old, Eliot, during a year in Paris, finished his now well-known poems "Portrait of a Lady" and "The Love Song of J. Alfred

Prufrock." He kept them in a notebook. Poetry was not his focus. He planned to attend graduate school and teach philosophy.[2] He gave a copy of his poems to a friend, the poet Conrad Aiken, however, and Aiken showed them to Ezra Pound. Pound said that Eliot's work was the best American poetry he had ever seen.[3] In 1914, the two met in London and

T. S. Eliot

began a collaboration that changed American poetry. "The Love Song of J. Alfred Prufrock" appeared in *Poetry* in June 1915 and marked the start of Eliot's career.

Eliot's life changed again when he fell in love with Vivien Haigh-Wood. Only a few months after meeting her he decided to get married and to live in London. They had a terrible marriage. She was in poor health, and Eliot suffered from insomnia, anxiety, and depression. During the years 1917–1925, Eliot wrote in the early mornings and worked as a clerk at Lloyds Bank. In the evenings, he edited a magazine, wrote reviews, and taught a night class on Victorian literature. He felt overworked and exhausted. In 1921, after a trying visit from his mother, Eliot collapsed of a nervous disorder. Doctors prescribed rest. Eliot spent three months in Lausanne, Switzerland, under the care of an analyst.[4] During this quiet time, he finished his long poem "The Waste Land."

He went back to London, back to work, and sent "The Waste Land" to Pound, who drastically slashed sections he found unnecessary. In 1922, "The Waste Land" was published in the *Criterion*. It was later published in book form, with Eliot's end notes. In the decades following its publication, many scholars and readers came to consider "The Waste Land" the most important poem written in the twentieth century.

In 1927, Eliot became a British citizen. In 1932, he traveled to Harvard to give a series of lectures and separated from Vivien, though he never divorced her. Vivien entered a mental hospital in 1938 and died there in 1947. By 1950, Eliot was the most respected poet of the time. During those years, Eliot wrote plays and critical essays and worked for Faber and Faber, the most important publisher of poetry in England. Eliot's editorial influence shaped British poetry for decades.

In 1948, Eliot became the only American poet ever to earn the prestigious Nobel Prize for Literature. In 1957, Eliot married again. He found happiness with his new wife Valerie that he had never had with Vivien. He died in London at age seventy-seven.

Preludes

I

The winter evening settles down
With smell of steaks in passageways.
Six o'clock.
The burnt-out ends of smoky days.
And now a gusty shower wraps
The grimy scraps
Of withered leaves about your feet
And newspapers from vacant lots;
The showers beat
On broken blinds and chimney-pots,
And at the corner of the street
A lonely cab-horse steams and stamps.
And then the lighting of the lamps.

II

The morning comes to consciousness
Of faint stale smells of beer
From the sawdust-trampled street
With all its muddy feet that press
To early coffee-stands.
With the other masquerades
That time resumes,
One thinks of all the hands
That are raising dingy shades
In a thousand furnished rooms.

III

You tossed a blanket from the bed,
You lay upon your back, and waited;

You dozed, and watched the night revealing
The thousand sordid images
Of which your soul was constituted;
They flickered against the ceiling.
And when all the world came back
And the light crept up between the shutters,
And you heard the sparrows in the gutters,
You had such a vision of the street
As the street hardly understands;
Sitting along the bed's edge, where
You curled the papers from your hair,
Or clasped the yellow soles of feet
In the palms of both soiled hands.

IV

His soul stretched tight across the skies
That fade behind a city block,
Or trampled by insistent feet
At four and five and six o'clock;
And short square fingers stuffing pipes,
And evening newspapers, and eyes
Assured of certain certainties,
The conscience of a blackened street
Impatient to assume the world.

I am moved by fancies that are curled
Around these images, and cling:
The notion of some infinitely gentle
Infinitely suffering thing.

Wipe your hand across your mouth, and laugh;
The worlds revolve like ancient women
Gathering fuel in vacant lots.

Summary and Explication: "Preludes"

As with other poems of Eliot's, "Preludes" is a collage, a larger piece created from fragments. Eliot links four preludes to create one poem. The word *prelude* means introduction, opening, or beginning. It is often used in relation to music, a short musical introduction to a larger composition. A prelude establishes tone and mood and is sometimes improvisational or free-form.

"Preludes" does not tell a narrative story. It captures an emotional reality through a series of images. The speaker describes images of the city as he strolls around or sits in an apartment. Night becomes day.

Poetic Technique

"Preludes" first appeared with the help of Ezra Pound in *Blast* in 1915, the same year as "The Love Song of J. Alfred Prufrock." They also share a similar style. There is no strict rhyme or meter, but Eliot uses mainly musical, four-beat, end-rhyming lines.

"Preludes" is melancholy because of its bleak imagery and its grim language. The adjectives alone, like *grimy, withered,* and *vacant* in section I, and *stale, dingy,* and *sordid* in section II, are enough to create the mood of this poem. The images are lonely, like newspapers blowing around in the rain.

Theme

Eliot often wrote about profound and basic themes of life, death, and aging. Many of Eliot's poems begin with time. Prelude I takes place in the evening and in winter, time periods that can symbolize ending, even dying. Morning is not a happy renewal in Prelude II. Time is disoriented in Prelude III. It seems to be the middle of the night. In Prelude IV, "four and five and six o'clock" seems once again to refer to late afternoon.

The poem shifts point of view, from third, to second, to first person. There is no specific character in the poem. One image refers to a woman: "You curled the papers from your hair." In the fourth prelude Eliot uses a third-person "his" and to conclude the poem introduces a first-person speaker. The poem seems to describe nameless, faceless people lost in a big city where thousands coexist "in a thousand furnished rooms." Eliot may be describing his own experience. He may be talking about himself in the first, second, and third person.

The poem's final two stanzas clash emotionally. Eliot contrasts the poignancy of "the notion of some infinitely gentle / infinitely suffering thing," with a directive to laugh. His final simile offers a dark view of the world. It is emphasized by the abrupt ending. After "Gathering fuel in vacant lots," it seems like there could be one more line ending with a word that rhymes with "lots." Perhaps Eliot did not want this poem to end comfortably.

FACTS

Eliot on Broadway

T. S. Eliot's *Old Possum's Book of Practical Cats* inspired the musical *Cats* by Andrew Lloyd Webber, which ran on Broadway from 1982 until 2000, the second-longest running musical in history. As a result, *Old Possum's Book of Practical Cats* became the best-selling book of twentieth-century poetry.

The Rum Tum Tugger

The Rum Tum Tugger is a Curious Cat:
If you offer him pheasant he would rather have grouse.
If you put him in a house he would much prefer a flat,
If you put him in a flat then he'd rather have a house.
If you set him on a mouse then he only wants a rat,
If you set him on a rat then he'd rather chase a mouse.
Yes the Rum Tum Tugger is a Curious Cat—
    And there isn't any call for me to shout it:
      For he will do
      As he do do
        And there's no doing anything about it!

The Rum Tum Tugger is a terrible bore:
When you let him in, then he wants to be out;
He's always on the wrong side of every door,
And as soon as he's at home, then he'd like to get about.
He likes to lie in the bureau drawer,
But he makes such a fuss if he can't get out.
Yes the Rum Tum Tugger is a Curious Cat—
    And there isn't any use for you to doubt it:
      For he will do
      As he do do
        And there's no doing anything about it!

The Rum Tum Tugger is a curious beast:
His disobliging ways are a matter of habit.
If you offer him fish then he always wants a feast;
When there isn't any fish then he won't eat rabbit.
If you offer him cream then he sniffs and sneers,
For he only likes what he finds for himself;

So you'll catch him in it right up to the ears,
If you put it away on the larder shelf.
The Rum Tum Tugger is artful and knowing,
The Rum Tum Tugger doesn't care for a cuddle;
But he'll leap on your lap in the middle of your sewing,
For there's nothing he enjoys like a horrible muddle.
Yes the Rum Tum Tugger is a Curious Cat—
   And there isn't any need for me to spout it:
    For he will do
    As he do do
      And there's no doing anything about it!

Excerpt from

The Love Song of J. Alfred Prufrock

Let us go then, you and I,
When the evening is spread out against the sky
Like a patient etherised upon a table;
Let us go, through certain half-deserted streets,
The muttering retreats
Of restless nights in one-night cheap hotels
And sawdust restaurants with oyster-shells:
Streets that follow like a tedious argument
Of insidious intent
To lead you to an overwhelming question …
Oh, do not ask, "What is it?"
Let us go and make our visit.

In the room the women come and go
Talking of Michelangelo.

ELiOT's PoeTic STYLe

Eliot found no living poets writing in English who inspired him. He had no one to model his work after. No poet had captured the modern world or any concerns about industrialism, war, and rapid change. Eliot found old romantic traditions meaningless, restrictive, and stuffy.[5] He found inspiration in the poetry of French symbolism. In college, in 1908, he read a book that changed his life called *The Symbolist Movement in Literature* by Arthur Symons. French symbolists expressed the unconscious mind with fragmented images.[6] This was a style that matched his view of the world.

Eliot wrote about profound, universally human themes—love, finding meaning in life, aging, and death. He often used the dramatic interior monologue, and created personas, characters, to speak his poems. For example, the speaker in "Gerontion" is an old man. The speaker in "The Love Song of J. Alfred Prufrock" is J. Alfred Prufrock, a figure some believe is a characterization of Eliot himself, an alter ego, a man he can gently mock. The critic Helen Vendler said it this way: "His Protestant ethical seriousness had to find a way to share its own idiom with his satiric irony, his sexual revulsion, his love of philosophical language, his desire for a musical line, and his exacting sense of structural form."[7]

Eliot kept a notebook full of fragments. He pieced them together to make long poems. This method created a new associative poetry that matched the collage style of modern art. It was a style that matched the chaos of the era of industry and war. No poem expressed the alienation of the modern world better or proved to be more important to modern poetry than "The Waste Land." Its publication in 1922, along with James Joyce's *Ulysses,* was considered the peak of modernism. The poem is nineteen pages long, with eight pages of endnotes. It has the two main ingredients of a modern poem: a fragmented form and a dark theme. Eliot claimed to write poems based on personal loss, anxiety, and despair. For readers, however, Eliot captured the uneasiness of the modern world, the isolation of big cities, and the enormous suffering of war. Eliot's poem represented the tremendous loneliness and despair of the modern world.[8]

Eliot wrote "The Waste Land," but Pound edited it by cutting whole sections he thought were old fashioned or did not flow with the music.[9] Pound liked difficult poetry. He believed a poem's obscurity was its power. Although Eliot worried that readers would not understand his poetry, he also knew that the point of "The Waste Land" was that no meaning could be found. Eliot asked important questions in his poems, but that did not mean he provided answers.

Once Eliot finished a poem, he never touched it again. Unlike his friend Marianne Moore, Eliot did not go back to revise or edit his poems after they were published. And, while some poets repeat a form or style over and over, Eliot never imitated the style of a completed poem. A new poem was a new beginning with new possibilities.[10] This creative habit may have disappointed readers who wanted more of the same. But Eliot saw life as constant change. He saw time as both destroyer and preserver. Eliot's poetry about time pulled the past and the future into the present.[11] He also never commented directly on his poems. He believed a poem meant whatever a reader got from it. Nonetheless, Eliot wrote important literary criticism, which indirectly taught readers how to read his poems. As a critical editor he had more influence on literary taste than any other poet.

What Critics Said

The publication of "The Waste Land" caused a storm. Young people read it out loud at parties or in their college dorm rooms. The poem created a new trend for students to imitate. Harriet Monroe explains the significance of Eliot's poem "The Waste Land" this way: "The agony and bitter splendor of modern life are in this poem, of that part of it which dies of despair while the world is building its next age."[12]

In 1922, some readers of "The Waste Land" were shocked by its grim, chaotic content. But William Carlos Williams was shocked for another reason. He said, "I felt at once that it had set me back twenty years."[13] Williams thought Eliot's poem was too academic, that it fought against the freedom that new poetry strove for. Because "The Waste Land" was so hard to understand and had so many footnotes, scholars and critics tried to create theories of meaning about it. Some said the poem was autobiographical, others said it reflected a decaying society, and still others claimed the poem was about spiritual rebirth. Eliot wrote very few books of poetry, but the number of books about his poetry is huge and continues to this day. There was no authorized biography written about Eliot, but there are some good unauthorized accounts of his life. Scholarship about his work was renewed when his second wife, Valerie, published his letters in 1971.

Though he wrote great poems at a young age, some scholars believe that Eliot's poetry matured as he became humble and vulnerable in his later work. His religious beliefs and Christianity also deeply influenced his writing. Louise Bogan wrote that in *Four Quartets* Eliot's voice, at last, was genuinely his own. All traces of persona and mask were gone.[14]

Major Works

Poetry

Prufrock and Other Observations (1917)

The Waste Land (1922)

Ash Wednesday (1930)

Old Possum's Book of Practical Cats (1939)

Burnt Norton (1941)

Four Quartets (1943)

The Complete Poems and Plays (1952)

Collected Poems (1962)

Essays

The Sacred Wood (1920)

The Use of Poetry and the Use of Criticism (1933)

Drama

Sweeney Agonistes (1932)

Murder in the Cathedral (1935)

The Cocktail Party (1950)

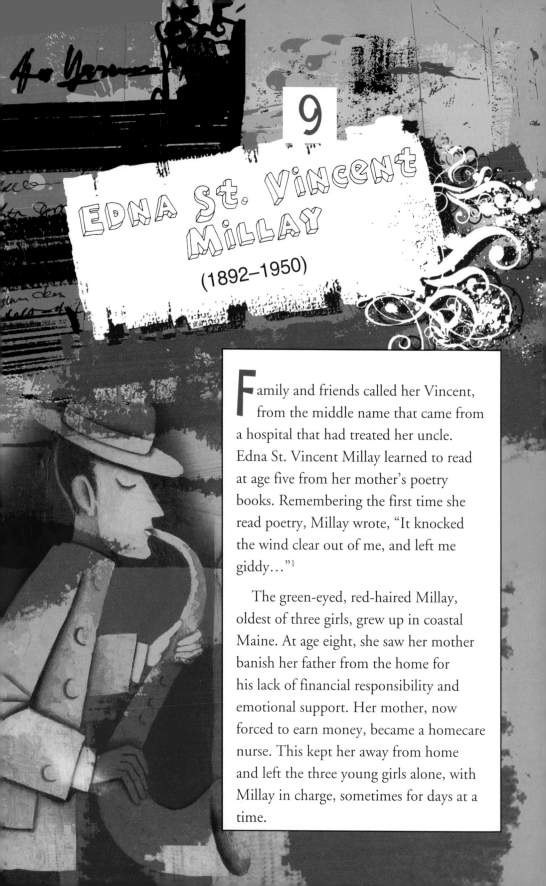

9

EDNA St. Vincent Millay

(1892–1950)

Family and friends called her Vincent, from the middle name that came from a hospital that had treated her uncle. Edna St. Vincent Millay learned to read at age five from her mother's poetry books. Remembering the first time she read poetry, Millay wrote, "It knocked the wind clear out of me, and left me giddy…"[1]

The green-eyed, red-haired Millay, oldest of three girls, grew up in coastal Maine. At age eight, she saw her mother banish her father from the home for his lack of financial responsibility and emotional support. Her mother, now forced to earn money, became a homecare nurse. This kept her away from home and left the three young girls alone, with Millay in charge, sometimes for days at a time.

Edna St. Vincent Millay

Millay's home responsibilities continued after high school. She could not afford college. She stayed home and kept house. At nineteen, feeling oppressed by housework, she entered her long, passionate poem "Renascence" into a contest, hoping to win the five hundred-dollar first prize. That single poem launched her to fame when it earned fourth place (though it was awarded no money). Readers, outraged that her poem had not won first place, instantly adored her. One wealthy woman, Caroline B. Dow, even offered to pay Millay's college tuition, sending her to Vassar, where Millay wrote poetry and acted in plays. She graduated in 1917.[2]

Millay moved to New York City and mingled with other artists. Everyone seemed to know who she was. People loved her poetry and saw her as free spirited. She represented the bohemian culture of Greenwich Village.[3] Her charm appealed to both men and women. Many people grew infatuated with her and pursued her company. Millay liked the attention, but she committed herself to her writing.

As Millay became successful, she continued to shoulder the burden of financial responsibility for her mother and sisters. To earn money, Millay published short stories and articles in magazines like *Vanity Fair* under the pseudonym "Nancy Boyd," her grandmother's maiden name.

In 1920, Millay sailed to Europe. She returned home just before she turned thirty-one. Her books *Renascence and Other Poems, A Few Figs from Thistles,* and *Second April* sold like hotcakes. That spring of 1923, after the publication of her fourth book, *The Harp Weaver,* Millay became the first woman to earn the Pulitzer Prize in poetry.[4]

Also in 1923, she married a Dutch businessman named Eugen Boissevain. He was forty-three; she was thirty-one. The couple bought a farm near Austerlitz, New York, and called it Steepletop after a wildflower.[5] Millay began to have health problems. Boissevain nurtured Millay back to health and cared for the practical details of their lives, allowing her time to write. Boissevain died in 1949, and the grief-stricken Millay never fully recovered. She died a year later at age fifty-eight.

Scrub

If I grow bitterly,
Like a gnarled and stunted tree,
Bearing harshly of my youth
Puckered fruit that sears the mouth;
If I make of my drawn boughs
An inhospitable house,
Out of which I never pry
Towards the water and the sky,
Under which I stand and hide
And hear the day go by outside;
It is that a wind too strong
Bent my back when I was young,
It is that I fear the rain
Lest it blister me again.

Summary and ExpLicaTion: "Scrub"

In "Scrub," a "gnarled and stunted tree" is a metaphor that describes the speaker's personal growth. She grew bitterly. She ate fruit that "seared," or burned, her mouth. She hid inside an "inhospitable house." These are descriptions of her emotional state rather than facts about her circumstances. In the last four lines, she explains why she is the way she is. She was hurt as a child. She uses the metaphor of harsh weather to describe her youth. The basic idea of the poem is that she was stunted because of the harsh conditions of her childhood.

We can assume the poem is about Millay herself. The poem's landscape sounds like the rocky, barren Maine coast where Millay grew up. Millay rarely complained about her childhood. She loved her mother and two sisters, and she loved the stark landscape that fueled her imagination. However, she must also have suffered. She had no father figure. Her mother often disappeared on nursing jobs, leaving Millay to take care of her younger sisters. They had few resources and sometimes went hungry.

PoeTic Technique

"Scrub," which appeared in *The Harp Weaver and Other Poems*, is a sonnet, a form that Millay perfected and used often. With shortened three-beat rather than five-beat lines, the poem's form reflects its content: It is a stunted sonnet about stunted growth.

Sonnets are composed of three four-line sections called quatrains and a final couplet. In "Scrub," the rhyme scheme of the quatrains is *aabb*. The first two quatrains pose a question, beginning with the word "if." When the speaker says, "If I grow bitterly," and "If I make … an inhospitable house," we know she will follow with reasons why. The last half of the third quatrain and the final couplet both respond with "It is that …" Then she provides the reason for her stunted growth: She was blistered by wind and rain, by harsh circumstances.

Theme

Millay often wrote about nature. She provides no factual information in "Scrub." The raw elements of nature symbolize the difficulties she endured as a child. Though the reader may feel raw emotion from this poem, the speaker seems to have accepted her "stunted" growth. She simply wants to explain it. Is she asking for compassion? Does she want to be understood or forgiven?

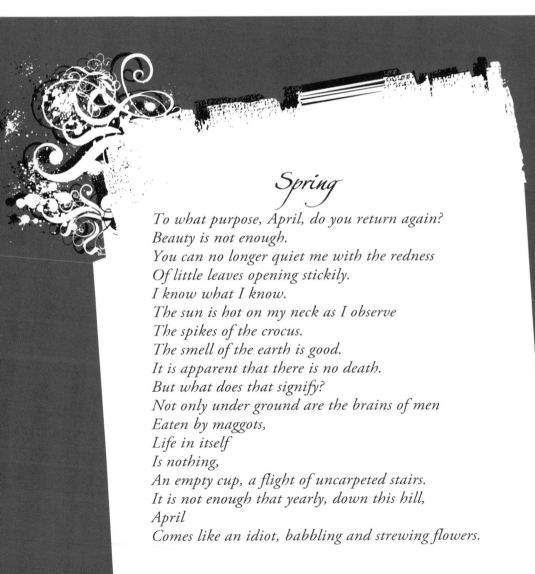

Spring

To what purpose, April, do you return again?
Beauty is not enough.
You can no longer quiet me with the redness
Of little leaves opening stickily.
I know what I know.
The sun is hot on my neck as I observe
The spikes of the crocus.
The smell of the earth is good.
It is apparent that there is no death.
But what does that signify?
Not only under ground are the brains of men
Eaten by maggots,
Life in itself
Is nothing,
An empty cup, a flight of uncarpeted stairs.
It is not enough that yearly, down this hill,
April
Comes like an idiot, babbling and strewing flowers.

Millay's Poetic Style

Millay published her major works at a young age and quickly became one of the most popular poets of her time. Biographer Nancy Milford wrote that Millay "found the three major themes in lyric poetry and made them her own: nature, love, and death."[6] She did not experiment with form or use free verse. She used the traditional rhyme and meter she had learned as a child. Her themes, rather than her forms, made her modern. She wrote about despair and loss and sorrow. She revealed an emotional honesty that many readers could relate to.

Millay used delicate imagery to describe nature. She wrote about love, but not idealized love. She did not describe traditional love relationships. Harriet Monroe praised Millay for "how neatly she upsets the carefully built walls of convention which men have set up around their Ideal Woman."[7]

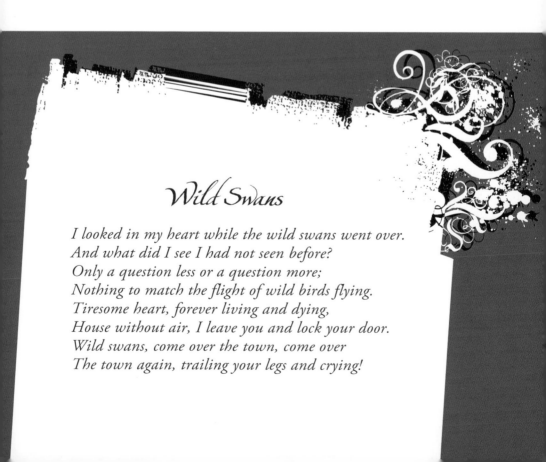

Wild Swans

I looked in my heart while the wild swans went over.
And what did I see I had not seen before?
Only a question less or a question more;
Nothing to match the flight of wild birds flying.
Tiresome heart, forever living and dying,
House without air, I leave you and lock your door.
Wild swans, come over the town, come over
The town again, trailing your legs and crying!

What Critics Said

Millay's first adult publication, her poem "Renascence," created a fury among readers. The poem earned high praise from critics such as Louis Untermeyer and was mentioned in *The New York Times* and the *Chicago Evening Post.* Readers of the poem compared her to Samuel Coleridge. They thought the author must be older, and male.[8]

In the 1920s, Millay became a sensation in literary as well as popular culture. She wrote for and was written about in the magazine *Vanity*

FACTS

Millay in the Village

The word *bohemian* was first used in France in the 1800s to describe unconventional or alternative lifestyles, especially of artists. Since the 1900s, the New York neighborhood most often labeled bohemian was Greenwich Village. In 1923–1924, Millay lived in the Village at 75½ Bedford Street, in the narrowest house in Manhattan (measuring nine and a half feet wide). Later residents included anthropologist Margaret Mead and actors John Barrymore and Cary Grant (though not all at the same time). Still a private residence, the house contains a plaque recording Millay's tenancy.

Fair. Countee Cullen, a poet of the Harlem Renaissance, wrote his undergraduate thesis on Millay.[9]

The poet Richard Eberhart called Millay "the finest American lyricist of the twentieth century."[10] In the era of Pound's maxim, "Make it new," Millay worked in traditional rhyme and meter. She did not write in modern free verse, but she did write about modern themes. Allen Tate called her "the one poet of our time who has successfully stood athwart two ages."[11]

Major Works

Renascence and Other Poems (1917)

A Few Figs from Thistles (1920)

Second April (1921)

The Harp Weaver and Other Poems (1923)

The Buck in the Snow (1928)

Fatal Interview (1931)

Wine From These Grapes (1934)

Huntsman, What Quarry? (1939)

Mine the Harvest (1954)

E. E. Cummings

(1894–1962)

Edward Estlin Cummings, called Estlin by his family, grew up in Cambridge, Massachusetts. His father taught English at Harvard and later became a Unitarian minister in Boston. As a boy, Cummings decided to write a poem a day, which he did for fourteen years. Though he later became very experimental, Cummings, like Pound, Eliot, and many other poets of the modern era, first studied traditional poetry and classical poets.

Cummings also studied Greek and other languages at Harvard, from 1911 to 1915, graduating with honors and receiving his master's degree in 1916. Intensely inspired by modern art, he delivered a commencement speech called "The New Art," praising modernism.

E. E. Cummings

Along with viewing visual art, he read Ezra Pound and other moderns and made friends with writers.

When World War I began, Cummings, a pacifist, volunteered for the noncombatant duty of driving an ambulance in France. It was an adventure. He got to see Paris. He was arrested by French censors, however, for refusing to testify against a friend accused of criticizing the French troops. Cummings spent three months in a French detention camp before being sent home to New York. To be arrested simply for being a man's friend fueled Cummings's rebellion against authority.

When he returned from duty, Cummings published his first poems in his new style. He also began a complicated affair with a married woman named Elaine Thayer. Elaine's husband almost encouraged the affair and remained friends with Cummings. Things got complicated, however, when Elaine got pregnant. Cummings's daughter Nancy, his only child, was born in December 1919. Cummings spent two and a half years in Europe, mainly in Paris, writing, painting, and studying art. In 1924, he returned to New York and married Elaine, but the couple divorced a year later. Elaine gave Nancy the last name of Thayer, and prevented Cummings from seeing her.

FACTS

Cummings the Artist

On the wall above her desk, Marianne Moore kept a small painting by Cummings of a yellow rose, her favorite flower. To see some of Cummings's paintings, look at the Modern American Poetry Web site.

During this time, Cummings wrote five books of poetry, a play, and many articles for *Vanity Fair*. His novel, *The Enormous Room* (1922), is based on his war experiences. His first book of poems, *Tulips and Chimneys* (1923), shows his originality and playfulness with language. He taught at Harvard, but quit after one year to devote his life to being an artist. He survived on grants, fellowships, and small family inheritances.

Cummings married again in 1929 and divorced in 1932. After the pain of two failed marriages, in 1934 he found stability with a photographer named Marion Morehouse. He lived with her until he died. The couple lived part of the time in a New York apartment and the rest of the time in his family's home in New Hampshire, a place he called "Joy Farm." The poems he wrote during those years reflect the contentment he had found in his personal life.

Meanwhile, his daughter, Nancy, had grown up and married one of Theodore Roosevelt's grandsons. Nancy admired Cummings's work but did not know he was her father. A friend introduced Cummings to Nancy. Overjoyed to be reunited with his daughter and to meet his grandchildren, Cummings wrote his most successful play, *Santa Claus*, a story about believing in love. In 1948, Cummings asked Nancy if he could paint her portrait. Over the months during which she sat for the painting, Cummings realized that she did not know he was her father. Finally he told her. They were both grateful to be reunited.

In the 1950s, Cummings began to give poetry readings and lectures about his life and poetry at colleges. He was wildly popular and entertaining. Based on lectures he delivered at Harvard, Cummings wrote a book of autobiographical essays called *i: six nonlectures*. He spent his last days on his farm. He was cremated and his ashes buried in Forest Hills Cemetery in Boston, Massachusetts.

In Just-

in Just-
spring   when the world is mud-
luscious the little
lame balloonman

whistles   far   and wee

and eddieandbill come
running from marbles and
piracies and it's
spring

when the world is puddle-wonderful

the queer
old balloonman whistles
far   and   wee
and bettyandisbel come dancing

from hop-scotch and jump-rope and

it's
spring
and
      the

            goat-footed

balloonMan   whistles
far
and
wee

Summary and Explication: Poem #30 "In JusT-"

The poem occurs in "just" spring. Four children, two boys and two girls, are called away from playing when a man Cummings calls the "balloonman" whistles. It seems as if the children are finished playing games. Playtime is over. Their names are significant. Notice that "eddieandbill" rhymes with "bettyandisbel." Because the names are strung together as one word, the reader wants to say them fast. It is interesting to note that Eddie is Cummings's first name and his father's, and Betty and Isbel are both nicknames for Elizabeth, his sister's name.

Poetic Technique

The poem progresses in three sections. The word *spring* appears three times, the balloonman "whistles far and wee" three times, and he is described with three different adjective phrases. First he is "the little lame balloonman," then "the queer old balloonman," and finally, "the goat-footed balloonMan." None of those descriptions seem entirely appealing. The balloonman sounds like a character in a myth or fairy tale. Whoever he is, he seems strange and a little scary. He may represent a satyr, the mythic goat-man who roams the woods dancing and playing the flute.

Cummings used only two capital letters in this poem—the first at the beginning, in the word Just. Maybe he wanted to emphasize a certain fairness or justice in nature's changes. The second capital letter is the *M* in the third use of the word "balloonMan." That *M* stands out among a whole poem of lowercase letters. Perhaps the evolution of balloonman to balloonMan represents the children's future adulthood. The poem could be about growing up.

Theme

Spring stirs up longings and memories, but its rebirth is a reminder of death. As soon as spring begins, it seems to end. Cummings often wrote about the seasons. He would never say, as T. S. Eliot does, in his first, famous line of "The Waste Land," that "April is the cruelest month."[1] Springtime was sweeter than that for Cummings. Spring meant youth and life and love. In this poem, spring seems to be joyous and nostalgic at the same time.

Everything new must eventually end—a day, springtime, childhood. As the poem ends, the words become more detached and farther apart. The words must be read more slowly. They look as if they should sound far away. The whole poem sounds wildly happy. The words could be shouted or sung. But the poem also seems to have a sad, wistful ending, as if a happy noise is fading and disappearing into the distance.

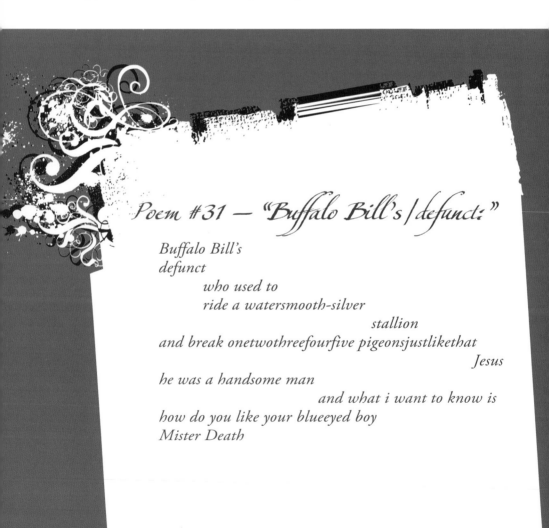

Poem #31 — "Buffalo Bill's / defunct:"

Buffalo Bill's
defunct
    who used to
    ride a watersmooth-silver
                 stallion
and break onetwothreefourfive pigeonsjustlikethat
                      Jesus
he was a handsome man
               and what i want to know is
how do you like your blueeyed boy
Mister Death

Discussion

"Buffalo Bill" is one of Cummings's earliest and one of his best known poems, first printed in 1919. The popular hero, Buffalo Bill, or William Frederick Cody, died in 1917. Notice that Buffalo Bill, though "defunct," seems like an animated cartoon hero. Why does the poem seem ironic?

E. E. Cummings was a painter as well as a poet. This is a self-portrait.

Poem #166 — "here's a little mouse)and"

here's a little mouse)and
what does he think about,i
wonder as over this
floor(quietly with

bright eyes)drifts(nobody
can tell because
Nobody knows,or why
jerks Here &,here,
gr(oo)ving the room's Silence)this like
a littlest
poem a
(with wee ears and see?

tail frisks)
                    (gonE)
"mouse",
             We are not the same you and

i,since here's a little he
or is
it It
?   (or was something we saw in the mirror)?

therefore we'll kiss;for maybe
what was Disappeared
into ourselves
who   (look).   ,startled

Cummings's Poetic Style

Cummings loved to paint as much as to write poetry. His poems, most of which he numbered, are highly visual. They cannot always be read aloud like most written work. For example, a line in #81 reads "bodyfee l inga ro undMe the traffic of." Remember, the typewriter was a new invention. For the first time, an author could place letters wherever he or she wanted. Cummings experimented with typography and made up his own rules. He used few capitals, referred to himself with a lower case "i," and deleted spaces after commas. He merged words or broke them into pieces. In some poems, half of one word sits on one line, the other half below it. Cummings sometimes put his name in lowercase and sometimes in uppercase. However, he indicated that publishers should capitalize his name conventionally. Most scholars carefully and respectfully cite his name as E. E. Cummings.

Cummings used language in a way that was startling and new at the time. He made adjectives into nouns, jumbled syntactical order, and used puns, slang, and hidden references.[2] He used the common language that Ezra Pound promoted. He wrote with a playful, childlike simplicity about earthy topics such as spring and love and sex and death. For example, Cummings begins Poem #95 with the line, "it is funny, you will be dead some day." This simple, surprising line might make a reader laugh or gasp or both.

With his combined experiments in form and language, Cummings crafted a unique style and voice. That style was important to him. It was specific to him, a style that readers were able to identify, and one that he used in all his writing.

He applied a childlike tone to his down-to-earth subject matter. He could convey a great sense of freedom by describing very small moments. Cummings had his share of loss and disappointment. He wanted to express the complexities of emotion, including hope and joy for life and love. He only wrote one review, of T. S. Eliot's *Poems*, in 1920. He also wrote a book called *Eimi* about a disillusioning visit to the USSR. Pound called it a masterpiece. For the most part, Cummings was not interested in critical, intellectual writing. Highly artistic, he preferred to focus on creating rather than studying.

WhaT CriTics Said

It took time for readers and critics to understand Cummings's style and themes. At first, some critics were annoyed and even angered by his use of irregular punctuation and his bawdy content. The same critics later praised his poetry for those same qualities.[3]

However, Cummings's first reviewers liked the way he experimented with form. They liked his inventive and original language. They saw the connection between his poems and modern art. His first publishers also appreciated his startling content, to a point. As much as readers of new modern poetry wanted fresh, honest poems about sex and death, they were also still easily shocked. Publishers chose poems carefully. They accepted the tamer poems and rejected the more shocking ones.[4]

Much later, however, some critics would complain that his style never changed from book to book. Cummings was very attached to his style. He has always been a more popular poet than critics give him credit for. Because Cummings was not an intellectual, some reviewers and critics did not take his work seriously. They found his work sentimental and naïve.[5]

Major Works

Poetry

Tulips and Chimneys (1923)

& (1925)

XLI Poems (1925)

ViVa (1931)

No Thanks (1935)

Tom (1935)

1/20 (1936)

Fifty Poems (1941)

1 x 1 (1944)

Xaipe: Seventy-One Poems (1950)

Ninety-five Poems (1958)

73 Poems (1962)

Complete Poems (1991)

Prose

The Enormous Room (1922)

Eimi (1933)

i: six nonlectures (1953)

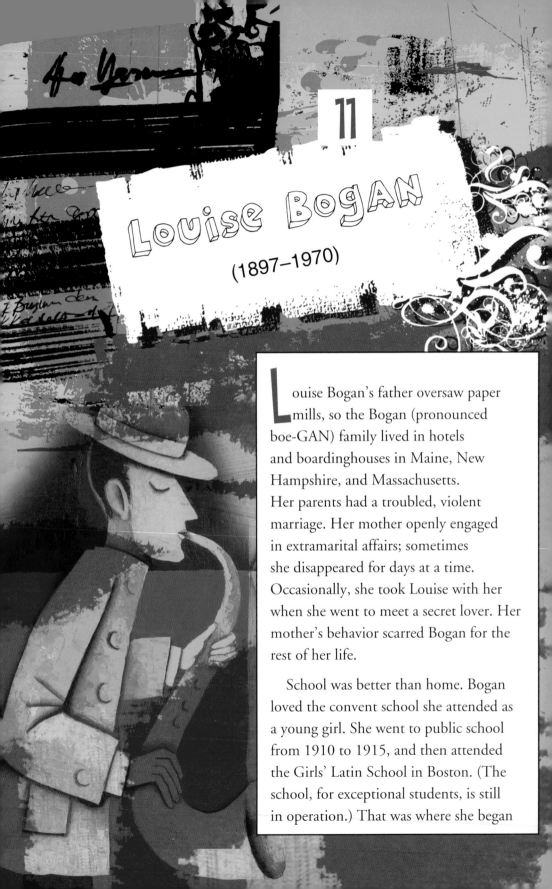

Louise Bogan

(1897–1970)

Louise Bogan's father oversaw paper
mills, so the Bogan (pronounced
boe-GAN) family lived in hotels
and boardinghouses in Maine, New
Hampshire, and Massachusetts.
Her parents had a troubled, violent
marriage. Her mother openly engaged
in extramarital affairs; sometimes
she disappeared for days at a time.
Occasionally, she took Louise with her
when she went to meet a secret lover. Her
mother's behavior scarred Bogan for the
rest of her life.

School was better than home. Bogan
loved the convent school she attended as
a young girl. She went to public school
from 1910 to 1915, and then attended
the Girls' Latin School in Boston. (The
school, for exceptional students, is still
in operation.) That was where she began

Louise Bogan

writing poetry. After high school, Bogan spent only one year at Boston University. She disappointed her family in 1916, when she turned down a scholarship to Radcliffe in order to get married.

Bogan's husband was a U.S. Army corporal serving in Panama. In 1917, Bogan went to South America to be with him. However, she was four months pregnant. The hot climate made her miserable. After delivering her child in 1918, she returned home. Leaving her daughter, Maidie, in the care of her parents, she moved to Manhattan on her own. Her brother was killed in battle in 1918, and her husband died of pneumonia in 1920, leaving Bogan a widow and a single mother at the age of twenty-three.

Her first book, *Body of This Death: Poems*, was published in 1923. The poems reveal her emotional grief but not the harsh details of her life. She had a bad childhood and suffered early loss as a young adult, and she was a talented lyric poet. Bogan was extremely private. Some of her friends did not even know she had a daughter. Much information about her childhood and family background is lost. She rarely talked about her problems, but she knew she could use her emotions in her poetry.

FACTS

Listen to Louise Bogan

You can hear a recording of Louise Bogan reading her poem "The Dragonfly" at the Web site of The Academy of American Poets.

Bogan remarried in 1925 to a wealthy writer named Raymond Holden, once a protégé of Robert Frost's. She had a strong marriage and a blossoming career. Unfortunately, her happiness would not last. A few months after her second book of poems, *Dark Summer*, was published in 1929, the couple's home burned to the ground. The poems Bogan had been working on were burnt to ashes. She never fully recovered her writing strength. She spent three months hospitalized for depression.

In 1931, she wrote a book review for *The New Yorker*. Little did she know that writing reviews would be her work for the rest of her life. In 1932, she traveled to Europe alone on a Guggenheim fellowship. When she returned, she knew her marriage was ending. She was voluntarily hospitalized again for depression, this time for seven months. In 1935, Bogan began a love affair with the poet Theodore Roethke. He was twenty-six; she was thirty-eight. The affair soon ended, but the relationship became a lifelong friendship. (When Roethke married in 1953, Bogan was the matron of honor.)

Her third book, *The Sleeping Fury*, was published in 1937. Like her earlier books, it was highly emotional but revealed no private details of her life. Bogan's three slim books would be her only original poetry. Throughout her life's writing, she revealed her sense of humor in letters to friends, including the writers Edmund Wilson, Rolfe Humphries, and Léonie Adams. During the last decades of her life, she became respected as an intelligent critic. She turned from poetry to prose, writing her autobiography, as well as reviews, essays, translations, and an insightful book about the modern era called *Achievement in American Poetry: 1900–1950*. Bogan died in her home of a heart attack in 1970 at the age of seventy-two.

Medusa

I had come to the house, in a cave of trees,
Facing a sheer sky.
Everything moved,—a bell hung ready to strike,
Sun and reflection wheeled by.

When the bare eyes were before me
And the hissing hair,
Held up at a window, seen through a door.
The stiff bald eyes, the serpents on the forehead
Formed in the air.

This is a dead scene forever now.
Nothing will ever stir.
The end will never brighten it more than this,
Nor the rain blur.

The water will always fall, and will not fall,
And the tipped bell make no sound.
The grass will always be growing for hay
Deep on the ground.

And I shall stand here like a shadow
Under the great balanced day,
My eyes on the yellow dust, that was lifting in the wind,
And does not drift away.

Summary and Explication: "Medusa"

In the Greek myth, the sea god Poseidon violates the beautiful Medusa in Athena's temple. Athena, appalled that her temple had been desecrated, turns Medusa into a Gorgon, a scaly beast with snakes for hair. Anyone who sees Medusa is turned to stone. The hero Perseus kills Medusa, uses her head to kill a sea-dragon, and gives the head to Athena. It is a story of intense transformation. Medusa is a woman (the root word of her name means wisdom) who becomes a monster who is then slain.

The poem reads like a dream. The speaker approaches a house. In dream imagery, a house represents the dreamer's psyche. The images are spare—trees, sky, a bell, the sun. Suddenly, in the second stanza, the speaker sees the horrible image of the beheaded monster. By the third stanza, the world has changed. It is a place where nothing moves. The words describe natural life like rain, grass, dust, and wind. However, the images are static, unmoving, and dead. They represent life, but they are not alive. The movement, like the yellow dust lifting in the wind, is as still as an image in art. By the end of the poem, the speaker herself is paralyzed. She is turned to stone, like Medusa's victims. She cannot look away. She suffers because of what she has seen.

Poetic Technique

Bogan knew that her one-word title would carry a lot of weight and provide context for her poem. "Medusa" is the title, but the name does not appear in the body of the poem. Even so, readers will have the context of her story in their minds from the start.

The poem has a careful sense of form. As in many of Bogan's poems, every word counts. Her language is careful and precise. "Medusa" has five stanzas. The first and third lines of the stanzas are long and the second and fourth lines rhyme. The longer, five-line stanza describes the Medusa and represents the moment of change. After that, each stanza is precise and the same, to represent an unchanging stillness.

Theme

Bogan wrote "Medusa" when she was only in her early twenties. Some critics, like Theodore Roethke, believe the poem reflects the childhood trauma that scarred her.[1] In that interpretation, Medusa may represent Bogan's mother, whose behavior damaged her psychologically. Another theory is that the myth of Medusa had personal significance for Bogan. Medusa, punished for her sexual behavior, was frightening but powerful, wise but monstrous. Bogan knew she had suffered trauma. She also knew she could create beauty from that personal trauma.

Knowledge

Now that I know
How passion warms little
Of flesh in the mould,
And treasure is brittle,—

I'll lie here and learn
How, over their ground,
Trees make a long shadow
And a light sound.

Discussion

"Knowledge" appeared in Bogan's first book, *Body of this Death*, which she published at the age of twenty-six. The poem speaks of the conflict between passion and reason, between the heart and the mind. It is a theme Bogan often wrote about in her poems, such as "The Alchemist." As a reserved woman, Bogan herself struggled with the conflict between passion and reason in her work and in her life.

Bogan's Poetic Style

Bogan kept the specific details of her personal life to herself. She believed that emotion rather than biography is what creates poetry.[2] In that sense, her poems are emotional biographies, not factual ones. They provide a map of her emotional life. As a poet, she believed she could absorb conflicts and express them creatively in a new way. Louise Dodd, in *The Veiled Mirror and the Woman Poet*, noticed that Bogan "emphasized her firm belief that the source of the lyric was personal emotion."[3]

Bogan did not write as freely as poets like E. E. Cummings or William Carlos Williams. She wrote in a more controlled way about the tug-of-war between the mind and the heart, a conflict she also felt in her life. She spoke honestly of her experience as a woman. Almost all of her poems address opposition. One theme of many of Bogan's poems is betrayal. The theme could spring from her early disappointment with love.

Bogan controlled her poems with form. She did not write in free verse, as other modern poets did. She used traditional rhyme and meter. She made precise word choices and used highly symbolic imagery. Her poems about love and grief are formal and spare but complex. She enjoyed reading difficult, obscure poetry. She believed those qualities created poems that could be read over again and again.[4]

"Women are not noted for terseness," wrote Marianne Moore, "But Louise Bogan's poetry is compactness compacted."[5] Bogan's poems were

The Alchemist

I burned my life, that I might find
A passion wholly of the mind,
Thought divorced from eye and bone,
Ecstasy come to breath alone.
I broke my life, to seek relief
From the flawed light of love and grief.

With mounting beat the utter fire
Charred existence and desire.
It died low, ceased its sudden thresh.
I had found unmysterious flesh—
Not the mind's avid substance—still
Passionate beyond the will.

short and concise, with emotion creating the intensity. Bogan tried to say the most in the least amount of space.

Body of This Death is a slim book—twenty-seven short poems. Her second book, *Dark Summer*, showed a maturity in her writing. In 1926, during a residency at Yaddo, an artists' colony in New York, Bogan wrote the title poem of her second book, "Dark Summer." The emotionally controlled poem deepened the direction of her poetry. By the time she published *The Sleeping Fury,* with twenty-five new, short poems, poetry had become difficult for her to write. Bogan turned to writing short stories and critical reviews.

WhaT CriTics Said

Reviewers and critics found Bogan's poems difficult and obscure. They liked the intensity of her language and form but did not always know what her poems meant. Some felt her craftsmanship outweighed her meaning.[6]

In her lifetime, Bogan became known more for criticism than poetry. Bogan's fans complained about how few poems she wrote. However, William Meredith reviewed *The Blue Estuaries* and wrote that Bogan was "one of the best women poets of the time."[7] W. H. Auden praised her poetry. Malcolm Cowley wrote that she "added a dozen or more to our small stock of memorable lyrics," something he said few of her peers had done.[8]

It was her dear friend Theodore Roethke who wrote the most widely read and quoted essay about Bogan. Using what he called Marianne Moore's "pointing out" method of criticism, Roethke wrote that Bogan's poems "can be read and reread: they keep yielding new meanings, as all good poetry should."[9] It is exactly what Louise Bogan wanted of her poetry.

Major Works

Poetry

Body of This Death (1923)

Dark Summer (1929)

The Sleeping Fury (1937)

The Blue Estuaries (1968)

Prose

A Poet's Alphabet: Reflections on the Literary Art and Vocation (1970)

What the Woman Lived: Selected Letters of Louise Bogan, 1920–1970 (1973)

Journey Around My Room: The Autobiography of Louise Bogan (1980)

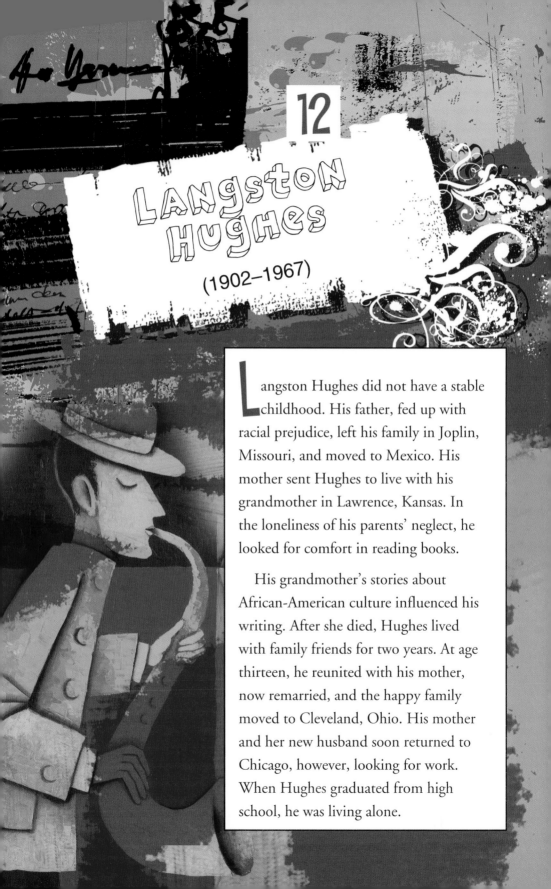

12

LANGSTON HUGHES

(1902–1967)

Langston Hughes did not have a stable childhood. His father, fed up with racial prejudice, left his family in Joplin, Missouri, and moved to Mexico. His mother sent Hughes to live with his grandmother in Lawrence, Kansas. In the loneliness of his parents' neglect, he looked for comfort in reading books.

His grandmother's stories about African-American culture influenced his writing. After she died, Hughes lived with family friends for two years. At age thirteen, he reunited with his mother, now remarried, and the happy family moved to Cleveland, Ohio. His mother and her new husband soon returned to Chicago, however, looking for work. When Hughes graduated from high school, he was living alone.

After finishing high school, Hughes reconnected with his father in Mexico. On the way there, as his train crossed the Mississippi River, the seventeen-year old poet wrote his most famous poem, "The Negro Speaks of Rivers."

His father offered to pay for college if Hughes studied engineering. Hughes preferred writing and literature. He went to Columbia University,

Langston Hughes

but left after one year. However, that year in upper Manhattan introduced him to the most exciting aspect of his life—Harlem.

In 1923, he took a job on a ship's crew and sailed to Africa. Next, he lived in Paris, Venice, and Genoa. He wrote and published poems during and between travels. He published "The Negro Speaks of Rivers" in *The Crisis,* the magazine of the National Association for the Advancement of Colored People (NAACP), edited by the African-American author and civil rights activist W.E.B. Du Bois (1868–1963). In 1925, Hughes published his first book, *The Weary Blues.* He returned to college, graduating from Lincoln University in Pennsylvania in 1929.

During his life, Hughes wrote in every genre—poetry, short stories, nonfiction essays and history, children's books, novels, plays, and even musicals. He edited anthologies and, fluent in French and Spanish, worked to translate the words of other authors. Though his writing brought him fame and financial security enough to buy a house in Harlem, he called himself a "literary sharecropper" because he worked so hard for his success.[1]

Hughes had traveled to Mexico, France, Italy, Spain, and the Soviet Union. He was outspoken about his leftist views. For this, he was called to testify about his politics by Senator Joseph McCarthy, who accused many Americans of communism. Hughes wrote about this experience in his second autobiographical book, *I Wonder as I Wander.* Intimidated by the committee, Hughes kept many of his poems out of print. His *Collected Poems,* which show the full range of his genius and make plain his political commitments, was not printed until long after his death.

At age sixty-five, Hughes died in New York of complications following surgery for prostate cancer. The street he lived on, East 127th, was renamed Langston Hughes Place, and his home has been given landmark status by the city of New York.

Harlem

What happens to a dream deferred?

Does it dry up
like a raisin in the sun?
Or fester like a sore—
And then run?
Does it stink like rotten meat?
Or crust and sugar over—
like a syrupy sweet?

Maybe it just sags
like a heavy load.

Or does it explode?

Summary and Explication: "Harlem"

In "Harlem," the dream is *deferred*, set aside, postponed until later, delayed but not forgotten. Although the poem is called "Harlem," the real topic is the question the first line poses, "What happens to a dream deferred?" Each line presents an imagined possibility of what happens when any goal is set aside and unrealized. Each possibility is a question except for one. The single period-ending sentence, "Maybe it just sags like a heavy load," stands alone and describes how "a dream deferred" might feel.

The images in this emotional poem are disturbing and physical. They assault the senses of smell, taste, and touch. One image is of a wound that never heals, and three others are related to food—a dried-up raisin, rotten meat, and a "syrupy sweet." The repellant images may almost cause a physical nausea in a reader. Food represents nourishment but if not cared for properly food goes bad. Too much sweet is sickening. Deferring a dream is not healthy. It deprives the dreamer of health and essential nourishment.

Poetic Technique

Hughes wanted his short poem to get a powerful reaction from his readers. He engages the reader by asking questions. Questions force readers to want to answer them. The single period-ending sentence sounds intentionally heavy, dull, and flat. His use of the word "maybe" implies resignation or defeat. But Hughes does not end the poem in defeat. That flat line comes just before one more question that seems to rise from the depths of despair: "*Or does it explode?*" The forceful line is further emphasized by italics. And though it is a question, its direct tone and end placement imply a finality that says this is the answer to the initial question. This is what happens to a dream deferred. It explodes. Sometimes when people express anger, we say they "explode." Since this kind of exploding is an active expression and a release, Hughes may imply a certain sense of triumph. What do you think? How do you interpret the last line?

Theme

The short poem is called "Harlem" but no descriptive details in the poem reveal anything specific about the New York neighborhood where Hughes lived. In that way, Harlem is an idea and a force rather than simply a place. Hughes also does not define the dream of his poem. Perhaps he knew that those two words, *Harlem* and *dream,* were enough to create a powerful picture.

The poem was published in 1951, when Hughes was fifty-three. He had seen Harlem's renaissance, and he had seen Harlem's dream crumble. He had seen the city, and the country, fail to achieve harmony between black and white cultures. But that dream—the goal, the aspiration, and the desire to create a good life—was important to Hughes. He wrote about this theme in other poems such as "Dreams" and "Dream Variations."

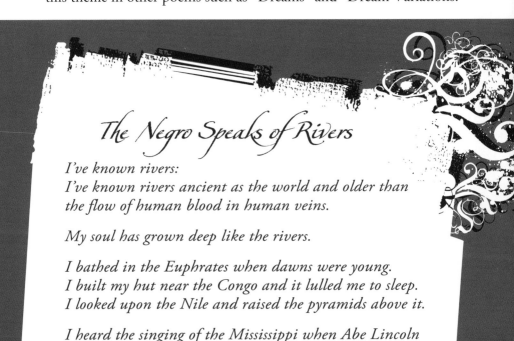

The Negro Speaks of Rivers

I've known rivers:
I've known rivers ancient as the world and older than
the flow of human blood in human veins.

My soul has grown deep like the rivers.

I bathed in the Euphrates when dawns were young.
I built my hut near the Congo and it lulled me to sleep.
I looked upon the Nile and raised the pyramids above it.

I heard the singing of the Mississippi when Abe Lincoln
went down to New Orleans, and I've seen its muddy
bosom turn all golden in the sunset.

I've known rivers:
Ancient, dusky rivers.

My soul has grown deep like the rivers.

I, Too

I, too, sing America.

I am the darker brother.
They send me to eat in the kitchen
When company comes,
But I laugh,
And eat well,
And grow strong.

Tomorrow,
I'll be at the table
When company comes.
Nobody'll dare
Say to me,
"Eat in the kitchen,"
Then.

Besides,
They'll see how beautiful I am
And be ashamed—

I, too, am America.

Hughes's Poetic Style

Hughes had one goal for his writing, to focus on his experience as an African American. He enjoyed being black. He loved his heritage. He loved black people. As a young man of twenty-eight, he wrote an essay called, "The Negro Artist and the Racial Mountain," in which he explained, "Most of my own poems are racial in theme and treatment, derived from the life I know."[2] He challenged other artists to embrace and express African-American culture rather than deny it.

Hughes believed writing had power and used his to expose racist attitudes. In his 1935 essay, "To Negro Writers" he wrote, "Negro writers can expose those white labor leaders who keep their unions closed against Negro workers and prevent the betterment of all workers. We can expose, too, the sick-sweet smile of organized religion—which lies about what it doesn't know, and about what it *does* know."[3] (Notice that he uses the same image of sweetness as he would fifteen years later in his poem "Harlem.")

Hughes's influences were Paul Laurence Dunbar (1872–1906), Carl Sandburg, and Walt Whitman (1819–1892), three poets who captured the dialect, or speech, of common Americans. Hughes used the language

FACTS

Hughes and Harlem

Learn about the important landmarks of Harlem in the 1920s and the Langston Hughes walking tour at the Web site of the Academy of American Poets. Watch a video of the poem "Harlem" on the Voices and Visions Web site.

Cross

My old man's a white old man
And my old mother's black.
If ever I cursed my white old man
I take my curses back.

If ever I cursed my black old mother
And wished she were in hell,
I'm sorry for that evil wish
And now I wish her well.

My old man died in a fine big house.
My ma died in a shack.
I wonder where I'm gonna die
Being neither white or black?

of the people of Harlem. Sandburg led Hughes to free verse.[4] Sandburg also influenced Hughes to use folk humor. In many comical, satiric short stories, Hughes found a new way to illustrate racism with humor through a popular fictional character named Jesse B. Simple. He wanted his writing to be clear and accessible. Like Sandburg, he wrote for the people he wrote about.

And like Sandburg, Hughes used the music of folk spirituals, blues, and jazz to inspire his poetry. Just as some of the modern poets applied the forms of modern art to their poems, Hughes applied the musical structure of jazz. In "The Negro Artist and the Racial Mountain" he wrote, "In many of [my poems] I try to grasp and hold some of the meanings and rhythms of jazz," and "Jazz to me is one of the inherent expressions of Negro life in America."[5] Some of the words of his poems sound like song lyrics. In fact, he wanted his poems to be set to music.[6]

What Critics Said

Some African-American critics condemned Hughes for focusing on lower-class black culture in his first two books of poetry. He wrote his essay "The Negro Artist and the Racial Mountain" in response to that reaction to his poetry. Hughes wanted his clear, simple poetry to make people think. W.E.B. Du Bois recognized Hughes's talent very early. When Hughes was only nineteen years old, he was regularly publishing his work. What is more, early on, students began writing research papers about his work. One student wrote a doctoral dissertation about Hughes in the 1930s.

In 1926, the African-American poet Countee Cullen wrote that Hughes's poems showed the "utter spontaneity and expression of a unique personality."[7] Reviewers recognized the brilliance of Hughes's dialect and the power of his simplicity. However, in 1959, James Baldwin accused Hughes of failing to live up to his skills and using a "fake simplicity."[8]

Poets of the Harlem Renaissance

In addition to Langston Hughes's poems, you may enjoy reading the work of the following poets:

Claude McKay (1889–1948)
Jean Toomer (1894–1967)
Countee Cullen (1903–1946)
Arna Wendell Bontemps (1902–1973)
Gwendolyn B. Bennett (1902–1981)

In spite of negative attention from critics, Hughes was prolific and enormously popular. That is why people called him "The Poet Laureate of the Negro" and "Shakespeare in Harlem."

Major Works

Poetry

Shakespeare in Harlem (1942)

Montage of a Dream Deferred (1951)

Short Stories

The Ways of White Folks (1934)

Autobiography

The Big Sea (1940)

I Wonder as I Wander (1956)

Introduction: Make It New

1. Harriet Monroe, *Poets and Their Art* (New York: Macmillan Company, 1932), p. 17.

2. T. S. Eliot, "Reflections on Vers Libre," *To Criticize the Critic and Other Writings by T. S. Eliot* (Lincoln, Neb., and London: University of Nebraska Press, 1991), p. 183.

3. Wallace Stevens, *Opus Posthumous* (New York: Vintage Books, 1989), p. 240.

4. Arthur, Symons, *The Symbolist Movement in Literature* (New York: E. P. Dutton & Co. 1919, 1958), p. 57.

Chapter 1. Robert Frost

1. William H. Pritchard, "Frost's Life and Career," *The Oxford Companion to Twentieth-Century Poetry in English* (Oxford University Press, 1994), <http://www.english.uiuc.edu/maps/poets/a_f/frost/life.htm> (November 12, 2007).

2. Robert Frost, letter to John T. Bartlett, July 4, 1913, in Dana Gioia, *Twentieth-Century American Poetics: Poets on the Art of Poetry* (New York: McGraw-Hill, 2004), p. 10.

3. Louise Bogan, *Achievement in American Poetry* (Chicago: Henry Regnery Company, 1951), p. 47.

Chapter 2. Carl Sandburg

1. Carl Sandburg, *Always The Young Strangers* (New York: Harcourt, Brace, and Co., 1952), p. 391.

2. Dana Gioia, David Mason, and Meg Schoerke, *Twentieth-Century American Poetry* (New York: McGraw-Hill, 2004), p. 110.

3. Richard Crowder, *Carl Sandburg* (New York: Twayne Publishers, Inc., 1964), p. 65.

4. Harriet Monroe, *Poets and Their Art* (New York: Macmillan Company, 1932), p. 36.

5. Carl Sandburg, *Selected Poems*, Christopher Moore, ed. (Avenel, N.J.: Gramercy Books, 1992), p. x.

6. Crowder, p. 63.

7. Carl Sandburg, *Harvest Poems 1910–1960* (New York: Harvest Books, 1960), pp. 5–7.

8. Sandburg, *Selected Poems*, pp. 5–10.

Chapter 3. Wallace Stevens

1. Milton J. Bates, *Wallace Stevens, A Mythology of Self* (Berkeley: University of California Press, 1985), p. 61.

2. Holly Stevens, *Souvenirs and Prophecies: the Young Wallace Stevens* (New York: Alfred A. Knopf, 1977), p. 48.

3. Bates, p. 65.

4. Dana Gioia, *Twentieth-Century American Poetry* (New York: McGraw-Hill, 2004), p. 119.

5. Carole Goldberg, "Poetry Lovers, Walk This Way," *Hartford Courant*, March 11, 2007, <http://www.hartfordinfo.org/issues/documents/artsandculture/htfd_courant_031107> (January 16, 2009).

6. Wallace Stevens, *Opus Posthumous* (New York: Vintage Books, Random House, 1989), p. 240.

7. Ibid., p. 242

8. "As Avant-Garde as the Rest of Them: An Introduction to the 1913 Armory Show," May 2001, <http://xroads.virginia.edu/~MUSEUM/Armory/intro.html> (January 16, 2009).

9. Louise Bogan, *A Poet's Alphabet: Reflections on the Literary Art and Vocation* (New York: McGraw-Hill, 1970), pp. 382–385.

10. Ruth Limmer, ed., *What the Woman Lived: Selected Letters of Louise Bogan, 1920–1970* (New York: Harcourt Brace Jovanovich, Inc., 1973), p. 121.

Chapter 4. William Carlos Williams

1. Dana Gioia, David Mason, and Meg Schoerke, *Twentieth-Century American Poetry* (New York: McGraw-Hill, 2004), p. 143.

2. "On 'The Great Figure'," Modern American Poetry, n.d., <http://www.english.illinois.edu/maps/poets/s_z/williams/figure.htm> (March 20, 2009).

3. Gioia, Mason, and Schoerke, p. 46.

4. A. Walton Litz and Christopher MacGowen, eds., *The Collected Poems of William Carlos Williams*, vol. 1, 1909–1939 (New York: New Directions, 1986), p. 266.

5. J. Hillis Miller, ed., *William Carlos Williams: a Collection of Critical Essays* (New York: Prentice-Hall, 1966), p. 17.

6. Litz and MacGowen, p. 188.

7. Ibid., p. 189.

8. Ibid., p. 199.

Chapter 5. Ezra Pound

1. Harriet Monroe, *Poets and Their Art* (New York: Macmillan Company, 1932), p. 12.

2. "Pound's 'A Retrospect'—Including 'A Few Dont's,'" *Modern American Poetry*, n.d., <http://www.english.uiuc.edu/maps/poets/m_r/pound/retrospect.htm> (August 6, 2008).

3. "On 'In a Station of the Metro,'" *Modern American Poetry*, n.d., <http://www.english.uiuc.edu/maps/poets/m_r/pound/metro.htm> (August 6, 2008).

4. Dana Gioia, David Mason, and Meg Schoerke, *Twentieth-Century American Poetry* (New York: McGraw-Hill, 2004), p. 168.

5. Charles Molesworth, *Marianne Moore: A Literary Life* (New York: Atheneum, Macmillan Publishing Company, 1980), p. 110.

6. Gioia, Mason, and Schoerke, p. 171.

7. Louise Bogan, *Achievement in American Poetry* (Chicago: Henry Regnery Company, 1951), p. 108.

Chapter 6. H. D.

1. Dana Gioia, David Mason, and Meg Schoerke, *Twentieth-Century American Poetry* (New York: McGraw-Hill, 2004), p. 203.

2. K. L. Goodwin, *The Influence of Ezra Pound* (London: Oxford University Press, 1966), p. 191.

3. Paul Lauter, ed., *The Heath Anthology of American Literature: Volume D, Modern Period 1910–1945* (Boston: Houghton Mifflin Company, 2006), p. 1225.

4. "D(oolittle), H(ilda) 1886–1961: Critical Essay by Harriet Monroe," *Book Rags, 2005–2006*, <http://www.bookrags.com/criticism/doolittle-hilda-18861961_1/> (August 19, 2008).

Chapter 7. Marianne Moore

1. Dana Gioia, David Mason, and Meg Schoerke, *Twentieth-Century American Poetry* (New York: McGraw-Hill, 2004), p. 227.

2. Charles Molesworth, *Marianne Moore: A Literary Life* (New York: Atheneum, Macmillan Publishing Company, 1980), p. 159.

3. Ibid., pp. 128 and 144.

4. George Plimpton, ed., *Poets at Work: The Paris Review Interviews* (New York: Penguin Books, 1989), p. 75.

5. Donald Hall, *Marianne Moore: The Cage and the Animal* (New York: Pegasus, 1970), p. 25.

6. Molesworth, p. 138.

7. Ibid., pp. 110–111.

8. "A Letter to Ezra Pound, from Marianne Moore," Jan. 9, 1919, in *Marianne Moore: A Collection of Critical Essays,* Charles Tomlinson, ed. (Englewood Cliffs, N.J.: Prentice-Hall, 1969), p. 17; and Molesworth, pp.134–135.

9. "The Marianne Moore Collection: General Introduction," The Rosenbach Museum and Library, n.d., <http://www.rosenbach.org/collections/categories/moore_collection.pdf> (July 11, 2008).

10. Molesworth, p. 169.

11. "The Art of Poetry: Donald Hall," *The Paris Review*, No. 43, Issue 120, Fall, 1991, <http://www.theparisreview.org/media/2163_HALL.pdf> (March 9, 2009).

12. Hall, p. 13.

13. Jeredith Merrin, "Marianne Moore and Elizabeth Bishop," Jay Parini, ed., *The Columbia History of American Poetry* (New York: Columbia University Press, 1993), p. 360.

14. Wallace Stevens, *Opus Posthumous*, Milton J. Bates, ed. (New York: Vintage Books, Random House, 1989), p. 217.

15. Hall, p. 47.

16. Ibid., p. 20.

17. Merrin, p. 343.

18. Louise Bogan, *Achievement in American Poetry* (Chicago: Henry Regnery Company, 1951), p. 58.

19. Stephen Bert, "Paper Trail: The True Legacy of Marianne Moore, Modernist Monument," *Slate Magazine*, November 11, 2003, <http://www.slate.com/id/2091081> (January 16, 2009).

20. Hall, p. 46.

21. Elaine Oswald and Robert L. Gale, "On Marianne Moore's Life and Career," Modern American Poetry, n.d., <http://www.english.illinois.edu/Maps/poets/m_r/moore/life.htm> (March 16, 2009).

22. Bogan, p. 58.

Chapter 8. T. S. Eliot

1. John A. Garraty and Mark C. Carnes, eds., *American National Biography* (New York: Oxford University Press, 1999), <http://www.english.uiuc.edu/maps/poets/a_f/eliot/life.htm> (January 16, 2009).

2. Peter Ackroyd, *T. S. Eliot: A Life* (New York: Simon and Schuster, 1984), p. 46.

3. Ibid., p. 56.

4. Ibid., pp. 115–116.

5. Helen Vendler, *Coming of Age as a Poet: Milton, Keats, Eliot, Plath* (Cambridge, Mass.: Harvard University Press, 2003), p. 96.

6. Garraty and Carnes.

7. Vendler.

8. Linda W. Wagner, ed., *T. S. Eliot: A Collection of Criticism* (New York: McGraw-Hill Paperbacks: Contemporary Studies in Literature, 1974), pp. 4–5.

9. "On the Composition of *The Waste Land*," Modern American Poetry, n.d., <http://www.english.illinois.edu/maps/poets/a_f/eliot/composition.htm> (March 17, 2009).

10. Wagner, p. 134.

11. Ibid., p. 127.

12. Harriet Monroe, *Poets and Their Art* (New York: Macmillan, 1932), p. 105.

13. "William Carlos Williams," Poetry Foundation, n.d., <http://www.poetryfoundation.org/archive/poet.html?id=81496> (March 17, 2009).

14. Louise Bogan, *Achievement in American Poetry* (Chicago: Gateway, Henry Regnery Co., 1951), p. 106.

Chapter 9. Edna St. Vincent Millay

1. Nancy Milford, *Savage Beauty: The Life of Edna St. Vincent Millay* (New York: Random House, 2001), p. 24.

2. Ibid., pp. 114–116.

3. Nina Miller, *Making Love Modern: The Intimate Public Worlds of New York's Literary Women* (New York: Oxford University Press, 1999), pp. 16–17.

4. Dana Gioia, David Mason, and Meg Schoerke, *Twentieth-Century American Poetry* (New York: McGraw-Hill, 2004), p. 384.

5. Milford, p. 274.

6. Ibid., p. 81.

7. Harriet Monroe, *Poets and Their Art* (New York: the Macmillan Company, 1932), p. 66.

8. Milford, pp. 76 and 80.

9. Miller, p. 16.

10. Edna St. Vincent Millay, *Selected Poems*, Colin Falck, ed. (New York: HarperPerennial, 1992), p. xvi.

11. Ibid., p. xvii.

Chapter 10. E. E. Cummings

1. Norman Friedman, *e. e. cummings: the art of his poetry* (Baltimore: Johns Hopkins Press, 1960), p. 95.

2. Richard S. Kennedy, *Dreams in the Mirror: A Biography of E. E. Cummings* (New York: Liveright Publishing Corporation, 1980), p. 330.

3. Ibid., p. 253.

4. Ibid., p. 252.

5. Ian Hamilton, ed., *The Oxford Companion to Twentieth-century Poetry in English* (Oxford: Oxford University Press, 1994), <http://www.english.uiuc.edu/maps/poets/a_f/cummings/cummings_life.htm> (January 16, 2009).

Chapter 11. Louise Bogan

1. Theodore Roethke, "The Poetry of Louise Bogan," in Martha Collins, ed., *Critical Essays on Louise Bogan* (Boston: G. K. Hall and Co., 1984), p. 94.

2. Louise Dodd, *The Veiled Mirror and the Woman Poet: H. D., Louise Bogan, Elizabeth Bishop, and Louise Gluck* (Columbia: University of Missouri Press, 1992), p. 73.

3. Ibid., p. 72.

4. Martha Collins, ed., *Critical Essays on Louise Bogan* (Boston: G. K. Hall and Co., 1984), p. 3.

5. Marianne Moore, *Predilections* (New York: Viking Press, 1955), p. 130.

6. Collins, p. 4.

7. Elizabeth Frank, *Louise Bogan: A Portrait* (New York: Alfred A. Knopf, 1985), p. 409.

8. Dana Gioia, David Mason, and Meg Schoerke, *Twentieth-Century American Poetry* (New York: McGraw-Hill, 2004), p. 393.

9. Roethke.

Chapter 12. Langston Hughes

1. Arnold Rampersad, "Hughes' Life and Career," in *The Oxford Companion to African American Literature*, Oxford: Oxford University Press, 1997, <http://www.english.uiuc.edu/maps/poets/g_l/hughes/life.htm> (March 9, 2009).

2. Langston Hughes, "The Negro Artist and the Racial Mountain," in Dana Gioia, David Mason, and Meg Schoerke, *Twentieth-Century American Poetics: Poets on the Art of Poetry* (New York: McGraw-Hill, 2004), p. 148.

3. Langston Hughes, "To Negro Writers," Modern American Poetry, n.d., <http://www.english.uiuc.edu/maps/index.htm> (January 16, 2009).

4. Rampersad.

5. Hughes, "The Negro Artist and the Racial Mountain."

6. Ibid.

7. Henry Louis Gates, Jr., and K. A. Appiah, eds., *Langston Hughes: Critical Perspectives Past and Present* (New York: Amistad Press, Inc., 1993), p. 3.

8. Ibid., p. 37.

consonance—Harmony or agreement of sounds in words.

couplet—A pair of lines with end-rhyme.

cubism—A style of art that emphasizes abract structure.

end-rhyme—A pattern in which the last words in poetic lines rhyme.

foot—The basic unit of verse meter in poetry; a unit of syllables within a line.

free verse (vers libre)—Poetic lines composed without a set rhyme scheme or meter.

iambic—A poetic rhythm consisting of an unstressed syllable followed by a stressed syllable.

imagery—Figurative language.

imagist—A style of poetry that employs free verse and the patterns and rhythms of common speech.

male rhyme—Rhyme consisting of one syllable (quick/stick).

metaphor—A figure of speech in which a word is compared to another to suggest similarity between them.

meter—The measure of systematically arranged rhythm in poetry, based on the number of stressed and unstressed syllables in a line.

modernism—The twentieth-century movement in art and literature that broke with tradition to form new modes of expression.

pentameter—A line of verse with five metrical feet.

rhyme—Arrangement of words by the final sound or sounds; lines of poetry may rhyme within the line or more usually at its end with another line.

romanticism—A movement in art, music, and literature that emphasized emotion, nature, and the experience of common people.

sibilance— An "s" or "z" sound.

simile—A figure of speech in which two things are compared using the terms "like" or "as."

slant rhyme—A rhyme scheme in which the vowels or consonants of stressed syllables are identical, as in cane/blame and years/yours. Also called half-rhyme.

sonnet—A poem with fourteen lines of iambic pentameter verse, with a variety of rhyme patterns, based on an Italian form ("little song") made popular by Petrarch.

stanza—A verse or set of lines grouped together within a poem, like a paragraph in prose writing.

symbolism—A late nineteenth-century movement in French art and literature in which objects had symbolic meaning.

Further Reading

Bolin, Frances Schoonmaker, ed. *Poetry for Young People: Carl Sandburg*. New York: Sterling, 2008.

Bryant, Jen. *A River of Words: The Story of William Carlos Williams*. Grand Rapids, Mich.: Eerdmans Books for Young Readers, 2008.

Fagan, Deirdre. *Critical Companion to Robert Frost: A Literary Reference to His Life and Work*. New York: Facts on File, 2007.

Hemphill , Stephanie. *Your Own: A Verse Portrait of Sylvia Plath*. New York: Knopf, 2007.

Lathbury, Roger. *American Modernism (1910–1945)*. New York: Facts on File, 2006.

Parisi, Joseph, and Stephen Young, eds. *The Poetry Anthology*. Chicago: Ivan R. Dee, 2004.

Polonsky, Marc. *The Poetry Reader's Toolkit: A Guide to Reading and Understanding Poetry*. Lincolnwood, Ill.: NTC Publishing Group, 1998.

Wallace, Maurice. *Langston Hughes: The Harlem Renaissance*. New York: Marshall Cavendish Benchmark, 2007.

Internet Addresses

Academy of American Poets
<http://www.poets.org/index.php>

Favorite Poem Project
<http://www.favoritepoem.org/>

Poetry Foundation
<http://www.poetryfoundation.org>

INDEX

WGRL-DR YA
31057101350018
YA 813.54 LLANA
Llanas, Sheila Griffin
Modern American poetry,
"echoes and shadows"